KU-681-005

Contents

Preface

Having now opted in to the Social Chapter, where will the Labour government take us next in our relationship with the European Union? Not into EMU, evidently, until the twenty-first century. As a recent leader in *The Times* observed:

> '*Mr Blair will continue to be dogged, like every other post-war Prime Minister, by the questions about Europe.*'

The issues that bedevilled the last Conservative government are all explained clearly in this up-to-date new edition of Brian Hill's deservedly popular *European Union*. He both asks the questions and gives the answers. In addition, in this edition an extra chapter has been added on the enlargement of the EU to include the so-called 'transitional economies'.

The book is designed to prepare students for the modular paper 4385 of the University of Cambridge Local Examinations Syndicate.

Bryan Hurl
Series Editor

SM99010295
6100
£6.25
DTF T
(Hil)

S̶T̶UDIES ... OK ECON̶OMY

The European Union

043 533 0438

Heinemann Educational Publishers
Halley Court, Jordan Hill, Oxford OX2 8EJ
a division of Reed Educational & Professional Publishing Ltd

OXFORD BLANTYRE MELBOURNE
AUCKLAND IBADAN JOHANNESBURG
GABORONE PORTSMOUTH NH (US) CHICAGO

Heinemann is a registered trademark of Reed Educational & Professional
Publishing Ltd

First published in 1991 as *The European Community*
Second edition published in 1994 as *The European Union*
Third edition published 1998

02 01 00 99
10 9 8 7 6 5 4 3 2

British Library Cataloguing in Publication Data
A catalogue record for this book is available from the British Library

ISBN 0 435 33043 8

Typeset and illustrated by TechType, Abingdon, Oxon.
Printed and bound in Great Britain by Biddles Ltd, Guildford

Acknowlegements

The Publishers would like to thank the following for permission to reproduce copyright material:

Philip Allan Publishers for the article by M. J. Roarty from *Economic Review* (April 1993) on pp.
21–2; The Associated Examining board for questions on pp. 11, 56, 67; © *The Economist*,
London, for graphs on pp. 12–13 (24/7/93), 68 (30/9/95), and articles on pp. 15 (22/9/90), 25
(19/2/94), 48 (26/6/93); The *Guardian* for the article and map on pp. 56–7; The *Independent*
for the extract on p. 64; London Examinations, A division of Edexcel Foundation, for questions
on pp. 12–13, 21, 34–5, 47–9, 66, 67, 78–9, 85; Bill Martin for the adapted extract on pp. 78–9;
The Northern Examinations and Assessment Board for questions on pp. 34, 78; The
Nottingham Evening Post for the article on p. 29; The Office for Official Publications of the
European Communities for the statistics on pp. 3, 10, 27, 31, 43, 54, 64, 72, 74, 87, 88 and the
extract on p. 20; The Organisation for Economic Cooperation and Development for the data on
p. 3; Chris Riddell for the cartoons on pp. 59, 60; Baroness Thatcher for the article on p. 70; ©
Times Newspapers Limited for the articles on pp. 34–5 (2/9/95), 42 (21/3/94), 53 (22/12/93);
University of Cambridge Local Examinations Syndicate for questions on pp. 11, 21, 55, 56–7,
67-8, 85–6; Vocational Technologies Ltd (01483 579454) for the table on p. 61.

The publishers have made every effort to contact copyright holders. However, if any material
has been incorrectly acknowledged, the publishers will be pleased to correct this at the earliest
opportunity.

Introduction

Why was the Common Market founded? How does it work? Is it a good thing – especially for the UK? What is likely to happen next?

This book presents the facts in an attempt to help its readers to answer these questions. It begins by tracing the origins of the European Economic Community and examining how it has developed into the European Union.

The economic rationale underlying this economic integration is the gains to be obtained from the operation of the law of comparative advantage in a free market. But this is a 'textbook' theory, so does it really work in the real world? What about imperfections and market failures? In particular what about the infamous common agricultural policy which makes a mockery of the free market concept? Even if the common market does make everyone better off as economic theory suggests, are the gains equitably distributed?

While the current fifteen members are busy deepening the Community why are another dozen clamouring to enter – especially ten central and East European countries suddenly freed by the collapse of communism in 1989?

Twice in this century the larger members of the European Union have fought against each other in mutually destructive bloody wars. The human costs are incalculable, the economic costs are small in comparison, yet enormous. The integration of the economies of the fifteen member states has made old enemies into fellow workers and friends; so, by making war amongst its member nations unthinkable the Union must be a great success. But how does its economic performance compare with that of the USA or Japan?

Is the UK better off since joining the European Union? Is sovereignty given up or shared as integration proceeds? Should the Union be a looser arrangement of sovereign states benefiting from free trade without the shackles of supra-national policies?

Whilst UK politicians argue, European integration progresses inexorably. Economic and monetary union with a **European central bank** and a single currency are the next stage. The end of the process will be a United States of Europe, but *when* remains to be seen. Whether this is a good, bad or sad thing is a matter of opinion. Readers will have to make up their own minds.

Chapter One

Origins of the European Union

'... *to establish the foundations of an ever closer union among the European peoples* ...' Preamble to the Treaty of Rome

What is the European Community, often referred to as 'the Common Market'? It is a combination of fifteen European countries which have decided that their future well-being will be enhanced by their union. They are gradually evolving from independent sovereign states to a federation or 'United States of Europe'. This process of integration is both economic and political. *Whilst this book concentrates on the economic aspects, it must not be forgotten that the fundamental forces involved are political, and so – not surprisingly – are controversial.*

In this chapter the forces that have led to the creation of the Community are outlined briefly and its objectives are analysed against this background. Finally, the Community institutions and the way in which decisions are taken and implemented are examined.

Table 1 gives some basic data on the size and composition of the Community, and comparative data for the United States of America and Japan. As the latter two countries are the Community's major competitors they are included in some other tables later in the book.

Historical background

At the conclusion of the Second World War, Europe was devastated economically. It was also fundamentally politically divided into a communist East and a capitalist West. The West included Germany and Italy which, with Japan, had fought on one side in the war, whilst the opposing side, the Allies, had included much of the rest of continental Europe in addition to Russia, the USA and the British Empire. Soviet Russia and the USA were much larger and more powerful than any other country. Some West European countries feared that their weakened condition constituted a power vacuum which might be too tempting for their huge eastern neighbour. They came together in defence treaties and to cooperate in economic reconstruction.

In the immediate post-war years many economists and politicians produced plans for a better and more secure future. One of the most influential was the French economist **Jean Monnet**. He envisaged a united Europe in which union would bring peace and prosperity to an area where nationalistic division and rivalry had imposed a tradition

Table 1 The European Union in perspective, 1996

	Area (1000 km²)	Population (millions)	GDP (milliard Ecus)
Belgium	31	10.2	209
Denmark	43	5.2	136
Germany	357	81.8	1850
Greece	132	10.5	95
Spain	505	39.3	464
France	544	58.4	1217
Ireland	70	3.6	51
Italy	301	57.4	953
Luxembourg	3	0.4	13
Netherlands	41	15.5	308
Austria	84	8.0	180
Portugal	92	9.9	85
Finland	337	5.1	98
Sweden	450	8.9	197
United Kingdom	**244**	**58.7**	**855**
EU15	3234	373.0	6742
USA	9373	265.3	5785
Japan	378	125.4	3664

GDPs at current market prices and exchange rates. Germany is the reunified Germany. The order of countries in this and subsequent tables follows European convention, being alphabetical in the native language of each country, e.g. Germany is Deutschland, Spain is España, etc.

Sources: *European Economy 62,* 1996; *Main Economic Indicators,* OECD, 1993.

of war and misery. He was convinced that a worthwhile future for Europe required economic and political union. So he conceived union by degrees, moving gradually from economic cooperation to **economic integration**, ultimately with full **political union** as the desired end.

Monnet's vision was given practical expression through the efforts of skilled politicians such as Conrad Adenauer of Germany, Robert Schuman of France and Paul-Henri Spaak of Belgium. *What role did the UK play?* None! The UK emerged from the war as the only major West European country not to be conquered, greatly weakened but still a world power and still possessing an enormous Empire. The latter absorbed British political attention, particularly as the Empire was being turned into a Commonwealth as its members were given sovereignty over their own destinies. So the UK lost the opportunity of playing a leading role in shaping the new Europe.

The reorganized Europe was brought about by the efforts of six countries ('the Six'), these being France, West Germany, Italy, the Netherlands, Belgium and Luxembourg. In 1957 they signed the **Treaty of Rome**, establishing the **European Economic Community** (EEC) from 1 January 1958. In 1967 these three Communities were merged and the new entity was termed 'the **European Community**'.

Enlargement of the Community

Although the UK did not relish economic integration and the implied loss of sovereignty this entailed, it did see much sense in cooperation in terms of free trade. Along with other countries having similar attitudes – the traditionally neutral countries – the UK tried to avoid the economic isolation which being outside the EC implied, by forming a free trade area. The **European Free Trade Area** (EFTA) came into being under the Stockholm Convention, signed on 4 January 1960. Its signatories were the UK, Austria, Denmark, Norway, Portugal, Sweden and Switzerland. EFTA was confined to trade in manufactures.

By the early 1960s the British government had changed its attitude to the Community. The UK's relative decline as a world power and changing trading patterns convinced British politicians that membership of the Community was now desirable. So in 1961 the Conservative Prime Minister, Harold Macmillan, announced that the UK would apply to join, although this was not a popular move.

Complicated negotiations followed, but they failed after two years when the French President, General de Gaulle, expressed the opinion that Britain was not yet sufficiently European to be admitted. In a change of government, Labour came to power and in 1967 Prime Minister Harold Wilson announced a new membership application. By the end of the year General de Gaulle had again effectively vetoed UK membership by announcing that such an event would destroy the Community. However, in 1969 he resigned and the Six agreed to open negotiations with the UK, Denmark, Ireland and Norway. The first three subsequently became full members on 1 January 1973. Although Norwegian negotiations also succeeded, the Norwegian people rejected membership in a referendum.

Further enlargements added Greece in 1981, Portugal and Spain in 1986. All three countries had emerged from dictatorships immediately before making their applications to join, and saw the Community as offering political stability as well as economic benefits. In 1990, following the collapse of communism in eastern Europe, East Germany was reunited with West Germany. Finally, Austria, Finland and Sweden joined in 1995.

These various enlargements of the Community can be a source of confusion to the unwary, because obviously *Community data refer to a different mix of countries over time*. A useful, but unfortunately not universal, convention is to write EUR6, EUR9, EUR10, EUR12 and EUR15. In this book most data relate to EUR15 even for the early years – by the simple expedient of adding figures for the later members to earlier Community data.

Objectives of the European Economic Community

These are best expressed by quoting in full Article 2 of the Treaty of Rome:

> '*It shall be the aim of the Community, by establishing a Common Market and progressively approximating the economic policies of Member States, to promote throughout the Community a harmonious development of economic activities, a continuous and balanced expansion, an increased stability, an accelerated raising of the standard of living and closer relations between its Member States.*'

This article makes it clear that a common market is expected to be of economic benefit to its members. It ends by looking towards 'closer relations between its Member States', implying that economic progress will lead towards some degree of political integration. This is consistent with the vision of Monnet mentioned earlier.

Although the prime aims of the Community are naturally directed towards its own members, its founding fathers were not entirely inward-looking. Article 110 says that the Community intends to contribute

> '... *to the harmonious development of world trade, the progressive abolition of restrictions on international exchanges, and the lowering of customs barriers.*'

Article 237 states that any European state may apply to become a member of the Community.

What is a common market?

The economic principles are to be discussed in the next chapter. For the moment a brief answer is that it is a group of countries which have no trade barriers between its members, but with a common agreed trade policy towards third countries. *Goods, services, labour and capital can circulate freely within and between members as the forces of free competition dictate.*

Since one of the main functions of government is to intervene in the national economy, some coordination is essential to prevent the distortion of competitive forces by different government policies operating in the member states. Clearly this coordination requires organizing and the Community has special Community level institutions to do this.

Community institutions

There are four major bodies: the European Commission, the Council of Ministers, the European Parliament and the Court of Justice.

The **European Commission** is the civil service of the Community. It is the main initiator of policy proposals, which it drafts and then discusses with the Council of Ministers, the EU Parliament and a variety of interested parties. When policies have been decided it sees to their implementation as **Directives, Decisions** and **Regulations**. All three types of outcome have the force of law throughout member states – if they conflict with national legislation it is the Community law which must prevail.

- Directives take effect through national legislatures, which are required to produce their own laws along the prescribed policy lines; that is, the resultant laws are tailored to suit different national circumstances.
- A Decision is binding upon a named person, company or state.
- Regulations are more general, applying in an identical fashion throughout the Community.

When a policy has been agreed by the Council of Ministers, the Commission organizes its execution, often with the aid of national civil services. Indeed most of the day-to-day implementation of policies is in the hands of national civil servants acting virtually as agents of the Community. The Commission itself is too small to do anything more than supervise in this field. Far from being the vast 'Brussels bureaucracy' imagined by some nationalists, in fact all of the EU institutions together employ fewer than 25000 people – less than the number employed by many UK metropolitan borough councils.

The Commission has 20 members appointed by member states, each in charge of a major policy area. The professional civil servants working under them are divided into 26 **Directorates-General** (DGs). These are similar to ministries in the UK. Some of the big ones of immediate interest to economists are DG IV – Competition, DG VI – Agriculture, and DG VII – Transport.

The **Council of Ministers** is not a fixed body of individuals; its composition depends on the policy in question. For example, if the topic is agriculture it is comprised of the Ministers of Agriculture from each member state, for transport policy the Ministers of Transport form the Council. All decisions are taken by the Council of Ministers. They receive proposals from the Commission, they may instruct the Commission to formulate a particular policy, they adopt and amend policies. As the Council is formed of national politicians it is to be expected that much political 'horse trading' takes place which may result in agreements involving unrelated issues despite the best efforts of the Commission.

The **European Council** is a special council of heads of state or government which meets twice a year. This council takes the fundamental decisions of principle which determine the nature and direction of Community activities. Occasionally the European Council will set up an Intergovernmental Conference (IGC) which, over a period of months or even years, will look in great detail at a particular policy. For example, both the Single European Act and Treaty of European Union (discussed below) were hammered out by IGCs.

The **European Parliament** is a directly elected body of 626 members sitting in Strasbourg. It is largely a consultative body, receiving and commenting on Commission proposals before they are adopted by the Council. The latter can pass laws even if the Parliament disagrees with them. However, the Parliament does have some budgetary power and in particular can reject the Community draft budget, which it did in 1985, forcing a new budget to be formulated. It can also, by a two-thirds majority, dismiss the Commission, though it would have no say in the appointment of replacements.

The **Court of Justice** is based in Luxembourg. It has 15 judges, one from each member state. The Court's judgements are binding throughout the Community. Indeed member states or institutions can be taken to the Court by individuals, organizations, other institutions or other member states.

Decision-making and the Single European Act

The Treaty of Rome allowed for decisions to be reached by unanimous agreement during the early years of the Community. Later, with growing political and economic cohesion, decisions were to be reached through a system of qualified majority voting. In practice, member states were very reluctant to give up the power of veto which the unanimity rule implied. Getting the agreement of all member states was never easy and proved increasingly difficult as the Community was enlarged, so that policy initiatives necessary for the development of the Community were only agreed after protracted negotiations. By the early 1980s the Community seemed to be grinding to a halt.

Following much discussion in European Councils and the reports of special committees, it was agreed to 'relaunch' the Community via a **Single European Act** (SEA) which was signed by all member states in February 1986. This Act is of great economic and political significance. It amended the Treaty of Rome in an attempt to achieve that Treaty's original economic objective of free trade within the Community. This was to be done by abolishing all internal barriers to trade, producing a **Single Market** by the end of 1992. Achievement of this boost to the Community economy was made possible by dropping the unanimity rule for decisions which did not involve points of principle. Thus decisions in the commercial field were now to be reached by *qualified majority voting*.

The qualified majority voting system gives ten votes each to France, Italy, Germany and the UK, eight to Spain, five each to Belgium, Greece, the Netherlands and Portugal, four each to Austria and Sweden, three each to Denmark, Finland and Ireland, and two to Luxembourg. The total is 87, and 62 represents a qualified majority. Luxembourg has one vote per 200 000 population; at the other end of the scale the larger countries have one vote for several million people. The system is designed to make it difficult for the larger countries to *impose* their views on the smaller ones.

The SEA also committed the Community to progress towards **Economic and Monetary Union** (EMU), and politically to include foreign policy and security. In 1989 an IGC was set up to study EMU and make recommendations to the European Council planned for December 1991 in **Maastricht**.

Meanwhile the collapse of the USSR power bloc led to the reunification of Germany. This took place in 1990 by East Germany being absorbed into the Community. Many were concerned that the enlarged Germany would become introspective and so hinder the further development of the Community. Chancellor Kohl of Germany and President Mitterand of France responded to such worries by proposing that *EMU should be accompanied by political union*. Accordingly another IGC was set up to examine this, also to report to the European Council in Maastricht in 1991.

The Treaty of Maastricht

This is the popular name given to the **Treaty on European Union** (TEU) which was negotiated in the 1991 European Council. It further amended the Treaty of Rome and so had to be ratified by each of the twelve member states. Sovereignty implications were sufficiently controversial to make ratification by several members a slow and painful process. In the UK, the right wing of the ruling Conservative Party regarded the Treaty as highly undesirable and fought against it. Nevertheless, national ratifications completed, the Treaty was signed in 1992 and came into force on 1 November 1993. Its three main features are:

- economic, social and political extensions to the existing EC
- common foreign and security policy
- intergovernmental cooperation on justice and home affairs.

The latter two aspects are outside the institutional framework of the Community. The net effect of the Treaty is to add a significant political dimension to the EC, the expanded whole forming the European Union (EU). This new title will be used in the remainder of this book except in historical contexts.

The EU budget

Originally the EU **budget** was designed to be very different from national budgets in that its only purpose was to finance common policies and administration. So it did not involve taxation, borrowing, deficits, or most importantly the redistributive functions of a national budget.

The budget framework was agreed in 1970 and was fully operational by 1975. It then had three sources of income:

- customs duties on imports
- agricultural import levies
- a VAT element.

Under the system of common tariffs, **customs duties** and **levies** are collected at the point of entry regardless of the destination of the imports once within the EU. Thus imports to Germany which arrive at Rotterdam are subject to duty there; clearly it is more reasonable to pay such duties into a common budget than for them to accrue to the member country of the port of origin. Ten per cent of the duties and levies are assumed to be collection costs and are retained by the country of the port of origin.

It should be noted that the **VAT element** is *not* an EU tax, it only provides a basis for calculating member states' contributions to the budget. The Commission calculates the yield which a VAT on a uniform basis would provide if levied in each member country. So this element of the budget relates to a *notional* VAT. In 1970 the maximum rate of VAT was set at 1 per cent.

Budget problems and solutions

In 1984, spending on agriculture increased so much that expenditure seemed certain to exceed revenue. In the event the budget was saved by delaying some payments until the following year and by 'repayable advances' made by member states.

The 1984 crisis persuaded the Council of Ministers to agree to curb agricultural spending and to raise the VAT ceiling to 1.4 per cent from 1986.

The budget was close to exhaustion in 1986 and 1987, and in June 1988 it was agreed to add a fourth source of income (retrospectively from 1 January 1988). This is a **GNP-based contribution** from members. The VAT base was restricted to 55 per cent of GNP immediately, but total budgetary expenditure was to be allowed to rise to a maximum of 1.2 per cent of GNP by 1992. A further increase to a maximum of 1.27 per cent of GNP by 1999 was agreed in 1992. In a 1995 'rebalancing' of the budget the VAT base was reduced to 50 per cent of GNP with the rate falling to 1 per cent by 1999.

Thus the GNP-based contributions are set to increase whilst the VAT contributions decline. *The rebalancing is from VAT that is not related to ability to pay towards GNP-based payments, which are so related.* At the same time the growing importance of the structural funds (see Chapter 5), focused on the poorer member states, means that the EU budget is undertaking a significant **redistributive role**.

Table 2 outlines the main elements of the budget for 1996.

Table 2 The EU budget 1996 (million Ecus)

Expenditure		Revenue	
Agricultural price support	41 328	Agricultural levies	1 963
Structural funds	26 006	Customs duties	12 853
Research	3 097	VAT own resources	39 792
External action	4 718	GNP own resources	26 712
Administration	4 129	Other	568
Other	2 611		
Totals	81 888		81 888

Source: *European Economy 63,* 1997.

Conclusion

The UK threw away its first post-war opportunity to be a major force in the reshaping of Europe. Subsequently the UK and other countries joined the project, and are now part of a process of increasing integration, the 'ever closer union' called for in the Treaty of Rome.

KEY WORDS

Jean Monnet	European Council
Economic integration	European Parliament
Political union	Court of Justice
Treaty of Rome	Single European Act
European Economic Community	Single Market
	Economic and monetary union
European Community	Maastricht
European Free Trade Area	Treaty on European Union
European Commission	EU budget
Directives	Import duties
Decisions	Levies
Regulations	VAT element
Directorates-General	GNP-based contribution
Council of Ministers	Redistributive role

Essay topics

1. (a) In what ways has economic integration already occurred in the European Community? [12 marks]
   (b) Assess the economic issues involved in determining the future form of economic integration. [13 marks]
   [University of Cambridge Local Examinations Syndicate 1993]
2. How is Britain's contribution to the European Community budget determined? Is it reasonable to expect Britain to pay a larger contribution in future? [25 marks]
   [Oxford & Cambridge Schools Examination Board 1993]
3. (a) How can the principle of comparative advantage be used to explain some of the benefits the United Kingdom has derived from its membership of the European Union? [12 marks]
   (b) Discuss the view that, despite these benefits, membership of the European Union is damaging the performance of the United Kingdom economy. [13 marks]
   [Associated Examining Board 1997]

Data response question
The following task is based on a question set by the University of London Examinations and Assessment Council in 1996. Study the employment data for the countries given, taken from *The Economist* of July 1993. The figures for Germany are for the former West Germany. Then answer the questions.

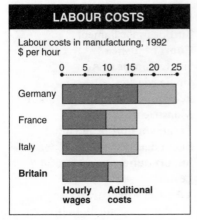

Figure A

Figure B

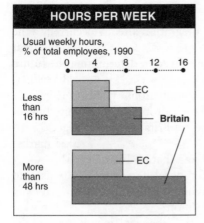

Figure C

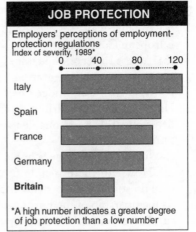

Figure D

Figure E   Figure F

1. With reference to Figure A, identify *two* major types of *additional* costs incurred by employers in hiring labour.   [2 marks]
2. With reference to Figure B, suggest *two* reasons which might explain the difference in participation ratios in the five countries.

[4 marks]
3. Examine the advantages of part-time work from the point of view of both employers and employees.   [4 marks]
4. (a) Assume a multinational company wishes to establish a new plant in Europe. With reference to the information available in the Figures, examine the factors which the company might consider relevant in choosing the location of this plant.   [6 marks]
(b) Examine *two* other factors which might influence the company in making its location decision.   [4 marks]

Chapter Two

Economic integration

'... the principle of comparative advantage ... is perhaps the most powerful idea in economics...' The Economist

This chapter attempts to answer the question – what are the economic benefits of a common market? On the theoretical side the gains from trade, due to the operation of comparative advantage, are analysed and related to different levels of economic integration. Finally, the expected size of gains to be achieved by the EU are discussed. This sets the scene for the remaining chapters which examine the activities of the EU in attempting to achieve these theoretical gains.

The gains from trade

Fundamental to any study of trade is David Ricardo's **Law of Comparative Advantage**. Most readers will be familiar with this law, but a thorough understanding should be ensured by studying the accompanying boxed article from *The Economist* of September 1990. Briefly, the law states that even if one country is absolutely more efficient in the production of every good than is some second country, if each country specializes in the production of the products in which it has a comparative advantage (i.e. greatest relative efficiency – it produces the goods it is best at producing), then trade will benefit both countries.

The benefits of trade due to comparative advantage are reinforced by economies of size (usually referred to incorrectly as economies of scale). This refers to the fact that, for many forms of production, average costs decline as output is expanded, at least until very large outputs are achieved. Specialization according to comparative advantage means that firms will have larger markets and will be enabled to grow larger, and hence have lower costs. This is a **dynamic process**, for large firms with low costs and high profits are able to invest in expensive research and development, *which enables these firms' productivity to continue to improve.* In fields of production involving complex modern technology only very large firms can afford to keep abreast of new developments and so compete successfully in world markets.

The most obvious gain from trade is the increased choice of goods for customers. If the UK had to be self-sufficient – unable for some reason to trade with other countries – the range of goods available would be greatly diminished. For example, it is possible to produce bananas

How to make comparative advantage work for you

These days politicians all over the world declare themselves in favour of *free trade*. When it comes to voting for it, they are not so sure. The reason is not just the pressure of special-interest politics. It is also that most people have imbibed the prejudice that free trade is a good thing, without imbibing the economics that ought to lie behind it. What this prejudice says, in fact, is that free trade is a good thing only if everybody else joins in; one-sided, or unilateral, free trade is a mug's game. The classical case for free trade argues exactly the opposite: *free trade is good for a country even if other countries do not return the favour.*

Writing 40 years before Ricardo, Adam Smith had already had a lot to say about the gains from trade. He saw it as, among other things, a way of promoting efficiency, both because it fostered competition and because it provided opportunities to specialise and gain economies of scale. Specialisation was a matter of absolute advantage: trade allows countries to produce what they are best at, and buy in the rest.

This view begged a question: what if Britain, say, is bad at making everything? Does this not mean that trade would drive all its producers out of business? David Ricardo answered the question by formulating the principle of comparative advantage. *This is perhaps the single most powerful idea in economics.*

Suppose there are two countries, Utopia and Flatland, and that these countries produce just two goods, wine and cheese. In Utopia it takes one hour of labour to make a pound of cheese and two hours to make a gallon of wine. In Flatland it takes six hours to make a pound of cheese and three hours to make a gallon of wine. Note that Utopia is more productive than Flatland in both goods; it has an absolute advantage in wine and cheese. But its greater

advantage, its comparative advantage, is in cheese. This will determine what happens when the two countries trade.

The precise outcome will depend on the pattern of demand, and hence on the price of each good in terms of the other once trade begins. Assume that a pound of cheese trades for a gallon of wine. This is for simplicity's sake; the argument does not turn on the price chosen. In Utopia, which is better at making both goods, an hour of labour can make either a pound of cheese or a gallon of wine. But since a pound of cheese can be traded for a gallon of wine, it makes sense for Utopia to specialise in producing cheese, and then trade some of its cheese for wine. In this way it can consume as much cheese as before and twice as much wine, or some combination of more wine and cheese.

Flatland is less efficient than Utopia at making both goods. But in Flatland too it pays to specialise. An hour of its labour can make one-sixth of a pound of cheese or one-third of a gallon of wine (which is worth one-third of a pound of cheese in the international market). So Flatland specialises in the production of wine, and trades some of its wine for cheese. Trade means that it can consume as much wine as before and twice as much cheese, or some combination of more of both.

The example has been borrowed, by the way, from an excellent textbook, *International Economics*, written by Paul Krugman and Maurice Obstfeld. In parts of the real world, though, the free-trade debate still seems to be struggling. Krugman and Obstfeld quote with amusement an article from the *Wall Street Journal* ('The coming overthrow of free trade') which observed, 'Many small countries have no comparative advantage in anything.'

Source: *The Economist,* 2 September 1990

in a hothouse, but only at such high cost that few would be able to buy them. If your breakfast today included cornflakes, and tea or coffee, what would you have had instead of these imported products?

Completely free trade benefits all participants, so why then is trade restricted by **tariffs** and other measures? There are four basic reasons:

- ignorance
- selfishness
- health
- strategic arguments.

Ignorance of the real economic facts is possible because decisions are not taken by economists but by politicians – often on the basis of a wide variety of fallacious economic arguments.

More likely is *selfishness*. Imagine that a major employer in your locality is suffering competition from imported goods and is consequently soon to become bankrupt. The local Member of Parliament persuades the government to intervene by assisting the uncompetitive firm. What assistance is likely? A subsidy would underline the firm's uncompetitive situation and so be inadvisable, but a tariff on imports would reduce or remove the imports (often described as 'unfair' competition) and raise prices, thus returning the firm to profitability and ensuring the jobs of its employees. But such a tariff is little different from a subsidy in that it enables an uncompetitive firm to survive. A major difference is that a subsidy is paid for by taxpayers, making it obvious and unacceptable, whilst a tariff is paid for by consumers through higher prices (and reduced supplies) which seem to go unnoticed. Clearly a tariff benefits a minority at the expense of society in general. Those about to go bankrupt or lose their jobs are vociferous, whilst consumers are more dispersed and unorganized and so make no effective complaint. Consequently protective tariffs are exceedingly common.

The third reason for trade barriers is to protect *public health*. Such trade restrictions are intended to ensure that imported canned products, for example, meet reasonable health standards, and clearly some measures of this type are justified.

Finally, *strategic* reasons for protective tariffs or subsidies refer to a country's need to safeguard its food supply, and manufacturing industries capable of producing guns, aircraft and ships in case of war; this is clearly not an economic justification.

Effects of tariff removal in a customs union

Referring to Figure 1, P_1 is the initial price in say the UK, domestic supply is Q_{S1} and consumption Q_{D1}. As a result of the removal of an import tariff after joining the customs union, the price falls to P_2 and consumption rises to Q_{D2} whilst domestically produced supply falls to Q_{S2}. Clearly consumers are better off because they now consume more of the good at a lower price. The resources which had been devoted to producing $Q_{S1} - Q_{S2}$ are released for the production of other goods.

Imports have increased from M_1 to M_2, the extra coming from another member or other members of the customs union where there is a comparative advantage in the production of this good. Similarly, for some other good for which the UK has a comparative advantage, tariff removal in other member states will provide the UK with an expanded market and the production of this other good will employ the resources released by the contraction of production of the first good. **Trade creation** is the term given to such cases; clearly it benefits all members of the customs union.

Trade diversion is a potential disadvantage of joining a customs union. Remember that when the tariffs on trade between members are removed, they are replaced by common tariffs between the group and the rest of the world. So the common external tariff may mean that a country buys a particular good from its fellow members although it previously imported it more cheaply from a third country. It is intuitively obvious that, provided that the common external tariff adopted is not higher on average than the previous tariffs of member states which it replaces, the gains from trade creation will exceed the losses from trade diversion.

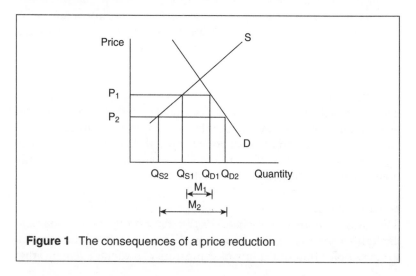

Figure 1 The consequences of a price reduction

This analysis has been conducted in terms of tariffs. Clearly the gains from tariff removal are applicable to the removal of any other forms of trade barriers.

Economic integration

There are five levels of economic integration between countries. *Inevitably each implies a degree of political integration which could be regarded as some pooling of sovereignty.*

• Preference areas

These are agreements to give privileged access to certain products from specified countries. Thus, following the Ottawa Conference of 1932, a system of Imperial Preference was introduced for trade between the UK and countries of the British Empire. This involved a **reciprocal reduction** of tariffs on trade between the participants, although tariffs against outsiders remained relatively high. Imperial Preference was designed to help the exports of agricultural products from the Empire to Britain, and the exports of British manufacturers to the Empire. The **Lomé convention** has since 1975 given preferential access to the EU market for some products of certain developing countries. In this instance the preferential treatment is one-way, and is regarded as a form of development aid.

• Free trade areas

Here, trade in an agreed list of products occurs freely between the members of the free trade area, although members retain their independent tariffs against third countries. *Such an arrangement is an attempt to gain the benefits of comparative advantage and specialization with a minimal loss of sovereignty.* The political content of an agreement is limited to rules which are necessary for its fair operation. The European Free Trade Area which the UK joined in 1960 is a good example (see Chapter 1).

• Customs union

This extends the free trade area idea to include a **common external tariff** against third countries. However, it involves far more political cooperation than does a free trade area. For example, the member states have to agree on the levels of tariff set and on their revision. This will obviously involve joint trade negotiations with third countries.

• Common market

This adds *freedom of movement for factors of production* (labour and capital) to the free trade in goods and services of a customs union. Proper application of the law of comparative advantage requires that there be no distortions to competition. Consequently much common policy formulation is required and so a great deal of political cooperation is essential.

- Economic and monetary union

A common market between member states having separate currencies still involves some internal trade barriers. These are **transactions costs** and **uncertainty**.

The former relate to the cost of buying and selling currencies which are obviously part of any trade in goods and services. Uncertainty arises because exchange rates can alter between the time when a deal is planned and the time when it is executed, and such a change may turn profit into loss.

The full exploitation of comparative advantage is only possible if there is a single currency. Thus economic and monetary union describes the situation when two or more countries unite their economies completely. *In turn this implies political union also,* for the effective control of an economy covers the money supply, taxation, the redistribution of incomes – in short, all the major economic decisions undertaken by a modern state.

Expected economic benefits of the EU

As discussed in the previous chapter, the removal of tariff barriers is a necessary but not sufficient condition for free trade. The EU failed to follow up its initial removal of tariffs on internal trade with the required complementary measures, and so after an initial decade of rapid growth, relative stagnation set in. The Single European Act was passed in 1986 to remedy this situation. It aimed at the removal of all trade barriers by the end of 1992 in a programme which is discussed in the next chapter.

As the accompanying boxed article from *Europe in Figures* indicates, the Single European Market was estimated to make the EU substantially better off. EU GDP and employment were predicted to increase whilst inflation would be slightly reduced. These are 'static benefits' – those that should be achieved within the first few years. In the long term the **dynamic benefit** was an expected increase of about one percentage point in the rate of economic growth. A 1996 Commission Report (COM(96) 520) estimates that the following benefits are directly attributable to the introduction of the Single Market:

- an extra 300–900 thousand jobs
- an extra increase in GDP of 1.1–1.5 per cent over the period 1987–93
- reduction in inflation rates of 1.0–1.5 percentage points.

The Single European Act

In December 1985, the European Council (the Heads of State or Government) meeting in Luxembourg, decided to give new impetus to European integration by drawing up a 'Single European Act', which was signed in February 1986 and came into force on 1 July 1987.

The Single Act is a new Treaty which modifies and supplements the Treaties of Paris and Rome (which established the three European Communities: ECSC, EEC, Euratom). Its aim is to bring the Community into line with the needs of the 1990s and to shape it into one large economic unit, a truly frontierless internal market with a population of 320 million: the biggest in the world.

Acting on the fact that Europe's lack of integration is proving expensive to the citizens of the Community (cost-ing between ECU 125 and 190 thousand million per year according to studies carried out by the Commission), the decision-makers in the Member States have decided to do everything possible to create, by 1 January 1993, a 'vast single market'. Citizens of the Twelve will be able to live and work in the country of their choice, regardless of what job they do. Tourists and travellers will be able to travel without frontier checks and use their credit cards in all the countries of the Community. Businesses will have a far wider market, leading to greater profitability from investment and the creation of employment – in short, an area in which there will be total freedom of movement for persons, goods and capital.

Source: *Europe in Figures*, 1989/90 edn, Eurostat

Conclusion

This chapter has concentrated on the theoretical gains from comparative advantage. The gains *expected* turn out to be impressively large, and the Commission study noted above suggests that these gains *can be achieved in practice*, but how has the EU attempted to capture them, and are the gains *equitably distributed*? We now turn to these questions in the next few chapters.

KEY WORDS	
Law of comparative advantage	Lomé convention
Economies of size	Common external tariff
Dynamic process	Transactions costs
Tariffs	Uncertainty
Trade creation	Single European Act
Trade diversion	Static benefits
Economic integration	Dynamic benefit
Reciprocal reduction	

Essay topics

1. (a) Why do countries join a customs union? [10 marks]
   (b) Comment on the implications of increasing the size of the European Union. [15 marks]
   [University of Cambridge Local Examinations Syndicate 1995]
2. (a) Explain why one would expect the Uruguay Round of GATT negotiations to have had an impact on specialization and on international trade. [50 marks]
   (b) (i) Why might there be gainers and losers from such a reduction in protectionism? (ii) Identify the likely gainers and losers.
   [30, 20 marks]
   [University of London Examinations and Assessment Council 1997]

Data response question

The following task is based on a question set by the University of London Examinations and Assessment Council in 1995. Read the article, which is adapted from 'The new protectionism and developing countries' by M. J. Roarty (*Economic Review*, April 1993). Then answer the questions.

Despite the success of GATT in reducing tariff barriers over the past 40 years, there is evidence of growing protectionism in the international trading system as shown by the proliferation of non-tariff barriers (NTBs). GATT lists over 1000 barriers, including quantitative restrictions (quotas and voluntary export restraints), pricing actions (anti-dumping and countervailing duties), technical and administrative requirements, and discriminatory public procurement policies. Anti-dumping duties and countervailing duties are imposed to restrict predatory competition or unfair trading.

Non-tariff barriers, although less conspicuous than tariffs, are potentially more damaging because they encourage bilateral trade deals which undermine the multilateral nature of GATT. The use of NTBs enables specific industries to be protected by targeting sensitive imports and trying to manage trade through bilateral arrangements.

As the economic climate has worsened in many countries, the number of trade restrictions has grown. There are several factors underlying this trend. First, a growing number of developing countries have achieved rapid, export-led growth by diversifying into manufactured goods. Export successes by these countries have meant import penetration deep into the heartland of industrial Europe and America.

Second, large trade imbalances between major trading nations have both strained international economic relations and had macroeconomic effects. This has led to claims of unfair trade and calls for retaliation against the guilty parties.

Another reason for growing protectionism has been the dramatic rise in unemployment in nearly all industrial countries over the past two decades.

As with all instruments of protection, there are significant opportunity costs in retaining resources in uncompetitive industries which only survive by shielding them from international competition. The burden of protection always falls on the luckless consumer, who is generally unaware of the price implications of trade barriers.

The other major 'losers' of the new protectionism are efficient producers abroad, especially developing countries, who suffer from trade diversion resulting in lost export revenues.

1. With reference to the first paragraph, explain how *two* of the non-tariff barriers mentioned would restrict imports. [4 marks]
2. Explain the suggestion that non-tariff barriers are 'more damaging' than tariffs. [4 marks]
3. (a) With reference to the passage, analyse the reasons which might explain the increase in non-tariff barriers. [6 marks]
   (b) Suggest *one* other factor which might also explain the increase in non-tariff barriers. [2 marks]
4. Explain why 'there are significant opportunity costs in retaining resources in uncompetitive industries which only survive by shielding them from international competition'. [4 marks]

Chapter Three

The Single Market

Non tariff barriers are effective trade barriers. Before the Single European Act it would have taken an accountant 50 years to qualify and requalify in each member country so as to be able to audit in each country!

This chapter examines how free competition within the EU – the Single Market – can be achieved; it involves removing many other impediments as well as tariffs on internal trade before goods and services can flow freely. The Single Market also has significant social implications which are also noted. Finally, as trade with the rest of the world is more important to the EU than to any other major bloc or country, it is appropriate to discuss here the attitude to competition in world markets.

Internal competition

It should be remembered that a common market involves the free movement of goods, services, capital and labour between a group of countries. Emphasis is to be laid on the word *free*, both here and in the term 'free competition'. *Only in a free market can comparative advantage, specialization and concomitant economies of size be attained.*

Economies of size in many fields of industrial production can be gained only by very large firms, much larger than those existing within the EU when it was formed. This implies either the growth of some firms, and the demise of their internal competitors, or their growth by merger and acquisition regardless of member state boundaries. Unfortunately the arrival of 'European firms' large enough to compete successfully in world markets with the largest American and Japanese firms requires the removal of national legal, technical and fiscal barriers by **harmonization** (an important EU concept which has sometimes threatened curious anomalies), *implying the replacement of national by Union-wide laws, standards and taxes.*

Harmonization in the industrial field has turned out to be extremely slow and difficult – this was one of the factors behind the introduction of the Single European Act (SEA) already mentioned, and discussed in detail below. The only significant industrial activity undertaken at Community level before the SEA was its assistance to declining industries, steel being the major example. The European steel industry suffered from chronic excess capacity and lack of international competitiveness. Its reduction in size and its modernization were coordinated by the EU, greatly assisted by the existence of the European Coal and Steel Community, which provided the necessary mechanisms.

Removing tariffs on internal trade is a necessary but not sufficient condition for free internal trade. A plethora of **non-tariff barriers** (NTBs) and state aids can effectively prevent or greatly reduce trade. NTBs include different technical standards and complex documentation. Before the Single Market, the manufacturer of a product might have to produce it in twelve different versions to satisfy different national criteria, and similarly provide different documentation for each member state, involving several languages. There are many other ways in which internal trade may be distorted, and the one which attracts most attention is *state aid*. Helping industries through the provision of production subsidies, artificially low interest rates, research and development expenditures and so on, may be legitimate (though economically dubious) government activities, but if practised differently by the individual member states competition will obviously be distorted.

Competition policy

The discussion so far has focused on national government policies, but private firms can also indulge in practices which distort **competition**. Price fixing and market sharing cartels are the prime examples. Indeed, the initiation of the 1992 Programme encouraged such a rash of mergers and acquisitions across national frontiers that some analysts asked if these were to capture the benefits of large-scale production or represented the cartelization of Europe.

National governments have long had their own measures to combat cartels. The Community leaves the control of cartels within member states to the members themselves unless there is an appreciable effect on trade between members. In the latter case *the Commission has wide powers to prohibit agreements intended to prevent, restrict or distort competition within the Single Market.*

Similarly, the Commission can prevent a firm which has a '**dominant position**' (e.g. a monopoly) from abusing that position. Note that having a dominant position is permitted – indeed the Community wishes to see more very large European firms capable of competing with the largest foreign firms in the world market; it is only the *abuse* of dominance which is prohibited.

Control over mergers and acquisitions which might give rise to a dominant position was agreed in 1989 along the following lines. Any firms whose desired merger seems likely to meet the regulation's criteria must notify the Commission of their proposals. The Commission will decide within one month whether to start proceedings and will then have four months in which to reach a final decision. Satisfying three criteria will cause the Commission to act:

- merging firms have a combined world turnover exceeding 5 billion Ecu (£3.6 billion)
- at least 250 million Ecu of turnover is generated within the EU
- less than two-thirds of the combined turnover comes from one member state.

The last criterion means that mergers with no major EU dimension remain the responsibility of national authorities such as the UK's Monopolies and Mergers Commission.

The EU Commission vets proposed mergers against the concept of a dominant position which significantly impedes effective competition. The regulation deals with any form of concentration of economic power and thus may include partial mergers and some joint ventures.

This regulation was reviewed in 1994. It remained unchanged despite the Commission's wish to extend its powers to mergers over 3 billion Ecu. The boxed article from *The Economist* of February 1994 gives an example of the policy in action.

A textbook cartel that broke all the rules

For months, Europe's unsubsidised steel makers have denounced the underhand way some governments finance their weaker brethren. Now they themselves have been found guilty of dirty tricks. On February 16th, in what he dubbed 'a textbook cartel case that broke every rule,' Karel Van Miert, the European Union's competition commissioner, announced record fines totalling 104m ecus ($117m) against 16 companies for rigging the market in steel beams.

The ringleaders in the cartel included British Steel (which was fined 32m ecus), and Unimetal, part of France's Usinor Sacilor group (12.3m ecus). According to Mr Van Miert, the steel makers used their cosy Brussels club, Eurofer, to put the cartel together virtually under the noses of his trust-busters. The steelmen also spun a web of bilateral deals among themselves, agreeing upon prices, staying out of each other's markets and exchanging confidential commercial information. The commission can fine firms up to 10% of their turnover in the market affected. The figure for British Steel was the equivalent of 7%, one of the highest rates ever imposed.

Source: *The Economist*, 19 February 1994

The Single European Act and 1992 Programme

In Chapter 1, the SEA was described as the 'relaunching' of the Community. It was necessitated by the effect of non-tariff barriers (NTBs) preventing the free movement of goods, services, capital and labour within the Community, and the slow progress made towards the removal of these barriers under the unanimity system of decision-making. In 1985 the European Council agreed to this Act to remove NTBs and create a single European market by the end of 1992.

The SEA amended the Treaty of Rome, and came into force on 1 July 1987. Since then NTBs have been progressively removed over a wide field, decisions being greatly speeded by the adoption of a system of majority voting (see Chapter 1).

Purchasing by governments and other public bodies accounts for about 15 per cent of the EU's GDP. Traditionally such purchases have been almost exclusively from national suppliers and contractors. As part of the **1992 Programme** such **public procurement** has been the subject of new directives which aim to ensure that all companies in the EU have a fair chance of tendering for such contracts regardless of national frontiers. These directives prohibit discriminatory specifications and complex tendering procedures, force major contracts to be advertised at EU level with reasonable time limits for bids to be received. Purchasers must be prepared to justify their rejection of bids, and complaints can be taken to the Court of Justice.

Electricity generating equipment and railway equipment are typical of the sectors most affected by these rules. Traditionally each national public authority favoured its national champions, with the consequence that intra-EU trade in such products was very small, price differences between member states were substantial and rates of capacity utilization were low. Clearly, because of the huge potential economies of size in these sectors, the single-market rules were expected to lead to a major restructuring through mergers, concentration, and closure of plants. Indeed the Single Market led to an immediate explosion of mergers and acquisitions both within and between states. Increasing concentration often enables firms to raise prices, but the increase in competition which the Single Market engendered has tended to reduce prices.

In the long term the EU aims to harmonize business laws and technical standards but this is a very slow process. In the short term some pragmatic changes have been introduced to free markets from legal and technical NTBs. Thus, a standard **Single European Document** has been introduced to accompany goods being sent across national frontiers, replacing a plethora of complex different national documents.

Most important on the technical front is the principle that what is acceptable in one member state must be acceptable in others. For example, in Germany, regulations insist that beer must be made from water, malt and hops only; all other additives are prohibited, and so

Germany refused to permit beer imports from other member states. The Court of Justice ruled that not withstanding their national rules, the Germans must permit the import of beers from other members – additives and all – provided that such beers met with the national standards in their countries of origin. This principle of **mutual recognition** is the key which has unlocked the door to the free movement of goods long before European standards can be agreed.

Financial services is one of the most rapidly growing sectors of the European economies but cross-frontier competition was prevented by NTBs. Consequently this sector was targeted in the 1992 Programme, and its liberalization was expected to contribute one-third of all the economic gains from the introduction of the Single Market. Two factors explain the lack of competiton in financial services.

- First, cross-frontier competition was impossible so long as national governments maintained capital exchange controls.
- Second, each government had its own regulatory framework.

Regulation in this sector is essential, to control the money supply for example, and to protect bank depositors from fraud.

The Treaty of Rome called for the free movement of goods, labour and *capital*, but for more than thirty years little was done to promote

Table 3 EU member states' trade with other members as a percentage of their total trade in 1958 and 1994

	Imports		Exports	
	1958	*1994*	*1958*	*1994*
Belgium/Luxembourg	56	68	55	72
Denmark	60	52	59	52
Germany*	36	51	38	49
Greece	54	64	51	54
Spain	32	64	47	65
France	28	65	31	61
Ireland	69	63	82	70
Italy	30	56	35	53
Netherlands	51	55	58	75
Portugal	53	71	39	75
United Kingdom	22	50	22	54
Total EUR 12	35	57	37	58

* 1958 West Germany, 1994 unified Germany.

Source: *European Economy 63*, 1997.

freedom for capital because of the autonomy of national monetary authorities and potential or actual balance of payments problems. However, in 1993 all controls on exchange and capital movements were removed. In 1994 a new EU banking licence system made it much easier for banks based in one state to open branches in other parts of the Community. Liberalization of the financial services sector has been much slower than intended under the Single Market Programme, and in 1996 the Commission noted the need for 'further measures'.

The gradual liberalization of intra-EU trade has brought about very large increases in trade between members countries. Table 3 provides the data to support this claim.

Tax harmonization

Article 99 of the Treaty of Rome called for the harmonization of indirect taxation, but the only major progress in this direction has been the adoption of value-added tax (VAT, based on the previous French system) as the method of collection. *The harmonization of rates of tax and excise duty is proving to be a particularly intractable problem, although members have committed themselves to this in principle as one of the provisions of the Single European Act.* Progress is hindered by the fact that all fiscal decisions are still subject to unanimity in the Council of Ministers. Differences in VAT rates are considerable and through their effect on market prices clearly distort competition. Rates of excise duties (on alcohol, tobacco and fuel) vary even more.

Different VAT and excise duty rates have resulted in member states having to maintain border formalities to collect taxes on imports and refund them on exports in intra-EU trade. Clearly this makes nonsense of the Single Market for many goods. In 1994, border formalities were replaced by other bureaucratic procedures to speed trade movements but it still leaves the distortions.

An obvious distortion is differences in excise duties on fuels which result in very different transport costs. The boxed extract from the *Nottingham Evening Post* takes a humorous look at the consequences of huge differences in member states' alcohol excise duties in the first year of the Single Market. In 1998 these distortions still remain.

Social aspects of competition

Initially social policy concentrated on retraining workers who became unemployed in the 1960s as a result of structural changes during this early period of rapid economic growth. More recently the **European Social Fund** has become one of the structural funds which are intended to help to redistribute more equitably the gains from freer

Get loaded on 'Booze Cruise'

C'est formidable. The French have finally revealed how much beer they sold the British this year – nearly 16 pints for every person of drinking age.

A year after cross-Channel trade barriers came down and the British began going to France en masse for cheap drink, the figures prove conclusively that Brits like their beer as much as the French like their wine. Especially at those prices.

Victory

The trend also poses a growing threat to the traditional British pub and off-licence, both of which are starting to feel the pinch now that one pint in every eight drunk at home is imported – legally or illegally – from France.

It is hard to say who can claim victory in the latterday Norman Conquest that has seen 120,000 Britons crossing the Channel each week from Dover to Calais.

It is certainly a mutually beneficial arrangement. The French hypermarkets rake in the cash from British beer buyers and the ferry companies are making a packet from the booming cross-Channel 'Booze Cruise', which transports 18 tons of beer back to Britain every day.

The drinkers have been saving a fortune in duty, while profiteers can cash in further by selling beer illegally at a profit back home – thanks to the law that allows unlimited amounts of beer to be brought over for 'personal use'.

How can Customs prove you are not buying a year's supply? The only definite losers are the Government, who charge 30p per pint in duty, compared with 4p in France.

The UK – Europe's second-cheapest producer of beer after Portugal – now charges the second highest rate of duty after Ireland, with one-third of the cost of every pint going to the Exchequer in duty and VAT.

So much beer is being brought in from France that no one can produce accurate figures. But wildly differing figures from each side of the Channel are both far higher than all pre-Christmas estimates.

The chamber of commerce in Calais estimates that 500 million litres of beer, wine and spirits have been sold so far this year, of which up to 80 per cent is beer. In English pub measures, that's 712 million pints.

The Brewers' Society estimates that a more conservative 150 million litres of beer – a mere 263 million pints – will have come in from France alone during 1993.

Output

But that is still more than the annual output of a British brewery like Youngs and Fullers, and the loss in excise duty to the Government will be around £240 million. With wine and spirits, the figure doubles to almost £500 million.

Brewers' Society spokesman Mike Ripley said: 'The problem is that we just pay too much tax on booze here.

'We are not just out of line with the rest of Europe, we are way out of line. And as long as there is that incentive, you will have people going abroad to buy it more cheaply'.

Source: *Nottingham Evening Post,* 1 January 1994

competition; this aspect of social policy is discussed as part of regional policy in Chapter 5. In the current chapter we are concerned with distortions of competition which may arise as a result of differing national social conditions, and rights of workers.

The Commission felt that the introduction of the single market, with its stimulation of business, should be balanced by the development of social conditions which would ensure that all citizens would benefit. The economic programme was to be given a 'human face'. Accordingly, the **Social Charter** was produced, its first draft appearing in May 1989. It was discussed in June by the Economic and Social Affairs Committee followed by the European Council. It was broadly welcomed by eleven member states but opposed by the UK. The Council made the following three points:

- In the construction of the Single Market, social aspects should be accorded the same importance as economic aspects.
- In the creation of the Single Market, job creation was to be given top priority.
- Implementation should comply with the principle of 'subsidiarity'.

The UK seized upon the term 'subsidiarity' and took it to heart, claiming that the whole topic was best dealt with by member states. The principle of subsidiarity, which the Social Charter introduced, was also included in Article 3B of the Treaty of Maastricht. It means that action should only be taken at the European level if a given objective could not be better achieved by member states. In theory the principle applies to all levels, thus national governments should allow local government to take decisions whenever possible. Whilst the UK government seized upon the principle eagerly insofar as it affected its dealings with the EU, it usually ignored it completely in its dealings with local government within the UK.

The Social Charter listed the 'fundamental rights' of EU workers, most of which already existed in the other member states, but several of which did not exist in the UK. For example there was no statutory right to annual paid leave in the UK, a right which already existed in all other member states except Italy. Similarly, only the UK and Denmark did not impose a limit on working hours (as publicity given to the hours worked by junior hospital workers may remind us). There was no statutory right to strike in the UK, and works councils were not compulsory.

The social concerns of the other member states produced a follow up to the Charter. They attempted to get its main provisions included in the Maastricht Treaty. Once again the UK refused and the outcome was a protocol to the Treaty.

Why was the UK government at that time so opposed to these social aspects of the EU? It claimed that implementation of the implied social policies would raise costs of production and make Europe uncompetitive. In support of these claims it noted that foreign countries' investment in Europe was being concentrated in the UK because of its refusal to adopt the EU's social aspirations. This was tantamount to admitting that the UK's attitude caused distortion to fair competition! But times and attitudes change – one of the first actions of the new Labour government elected in 1997 was to announce its intention to sign up to the EU's social policy.

What are the likely consequences of signing up to the social aspects of Maastricht? Probably nothing spectacular. Some of the major UK employers introduced works councils several years ago because they seemed to be successful in other member states. The attitude that co-operation is better than confrontation is one shared by the new government. However, its tough stance on welfare benefits suggests that any new rights will be tempered with appropriate responsibilities.

External trade

The EU is the world's largest trading group, as Table 4 shows (note that intra-EU trade is excluded from the table). External trade is about 10 per cent of the EU's GDP. Clearly no discussion of EU competition policy is complete without some consideration of the Union's position in world markets.

T a b l e   4   Share of EU in world trade, 1994 (percentages)

	Imports	Exports
EU	19.4	19.9
USA	20.6	15.9
Japan	8.2	12.3
China	3.5	3.7
Russia	1.2	1.9
Others	47.1	46.3

Source: *CEC: How does the European Union Relate to the World?* Brussels, 1996.

In 1947, the leading trading nations signed the **General Agreement on Tariffs and Trade** (GATT). This sought to avoid the protectionism of the 1930s which had greatly exacerbated the worldwide 'Great Depression'. Its main aim was to reduce trade barriers, though it excluded agriculture and services. Its crucial principle is the **most-**

favoured-nation clause; under this, a country agreeing a tariff reduction to one country is obliged to offer the same reduction to all GATT members. How can the EU countries with zero internal tariffs and a common external tariff against third countries belong to GATT? The latter's rules exempt customs unions and free trade areas from this non-discrimination rule *provided that their formation does not raise the tariffs of the new trade group to a level greater on average than the previous tariffs of the individual members.* It is also permissible to offer reduced tariffs on a discriminatory basis to developing countries.

In Article 110 of the Treaty of Rome, the Community states its intention of contributing to

> *'the harmonious development of world trade, the progressive abolition of restrictions on international exchanges and the lowering of customs barriers'*

To date the Community has three main discriminatory agreements: two are for reciprocal free trade in industrial products with the European Free Trade Area and ten Central and East European Countries (see Chapter 8); the other – the **Lomé Convention** – offers non-reciprocal tariff preferences for most non-agricultural goods and preferential access for some food products. The Lomé Convention covers 66 African, Caribbean and Pacific (ACP) countries, mostly the ex-colonies of EU members. In addition to trade preferences it also provides aid for the ACP countries with special funds to stabilize their export earnings, and a European Development Fund to finance development projects.

From time to time GATT members enter a round of international negotiations to try to liberalize trade. As the EU has a common trade policy the Commission represents it, though its agreements have to be ratified by the Council of Ministers.

Successive rounds of negotiations in GATT since 1947 give the impression that trade barriers have been progressively reduced since tariffs have certainly fallen to low levels. *The truth is that their place was taken by NTBs. Two examples underline the point.* The Multi-fibre Arrangements (between developed-country textile importers, notably EU, USA and Japan, and developing-country exporters) placed quantitative restrictions on trade. Similarly, the EU's large trade deficit with Japan led to the imposition of Voluntary Export Restraints (VERs) on a wide range of goods such as motor cars and electronic items. Such quantitative restrictions became common.

In 1985 it was agreed to launch a new round of trade negotiations, the **Uruguay Round** (since this is where the initial conference was held), to be completed by the end of 1990. As this round was to include agriculture in addition to tariffs and NTBs, it is not surprising that progress was slow. The main protagonists were the USA and the EU. The former is the world's major food exporter and had to compete in world markets with heavily subsidized European food exports (see Chapter 4). So the USA wanted to see the EU's agricultural policy remodelled to remove these dumped surpluses and offered to reform its own system of protecting agriculture. In the event, GATT negotiations ground on and on, not producing a new agreement until December 1993, almost three years beyond the original deadline. As will be examined in the next chapter, major agricultural concessions testify to the importance of trade to the EU.

In 1995 the name of GATT was changed to the World Trade Organization (WTO). Its role, methods and existing trade agreements remained unchanged.

Conclusion

Freer trade has been achieved both within the single market and with the rest of the world. In the single market the key has been mutual recognition. Mutual recognition applies to individuals, food, goods and services. for example, an accountant or any other professional who is qualified in one member state can work in any of the others. Liberalization of some sectors – financial services for example – is incomplete and likely to be subject to further measures. The lack of fiscal harmonization also remains as a major competition-distorting problem.

KEY WORDS

Harmonization	European central bank
Non-tariff barriers	Tax harmonization
Competition	European Social Fund
Dominant position	Social Charter
Single European Act	Social Chapter
1992 Programme	External trade
Public procurement	GATT
Single European Document	Most favoured nation
Mutual recognition	Uruguay Round
Subsidiarity	

Essay topic

How in theory should the single European market improve the economy of Europe? Discuss whether or not the benefits from these
improvements are likely to be shared equally by the participating
nations. [25 marks]

[Northern Examinations and Assessment Board 1995]

Data response question

The following task is based on a question set by the University of
London Examinations and Assessment Council in 1997. Read the article 'Holidays in France', which is adapted from a piece by S. Keenan
published in *The Times* on 2 September 1995. Then answer the questions.

Holidays in France

France is still pretty, yes. The food and ambience are appealing,
the beaches of the west coast sandy and great for kids. The
supermarket beer is cheap, and buying wine is essential for the
cellar back home.

But, oh, the woeful exchange rate! At the Carrefour hypermarkets at Cité Europe near Calais, Julie and her friend Linda, both
from Southampton, were returning from a five-day work/pleasure
trip to Rheims in the Champagne area. 'Prices were pretty grim',
admitted Linda, 'We drank half-bottles of wine instead of full bot-
tles. We also made a point of filling up with petrol in Dover.'

Petrol at Carrefour was selling for 74p a litre, compared with 60p
in Britain. Jeremy, his wife Jane and three children didn't fill up at
Dover. 'It cost us £10 a tank more', he sighed. With children aged
eight, six and three, the family had spent their normal two weeks on
a camp site at Carnac. 'Normally we would have one or two meals
out with the children, but this year we didn't eat or drink out.'

Staples like coffee and jam are now more expensive than at
home, they agreed. The spending budget of £500 had crept past
the £650 mark, with the final tally still dependent on the credit card
statement. Jane echoed the common remark: 'People still make
the mistake of dividing every price by 10 instead of 7.'

Indeed, the strong state of the franc has increasingly meant a
pound for sterling, worth Fr10 in 1992, Fr8 a year ago, and F7.6
last weekend. The French have raised accommodation prices this
summer and also VAT to 20.2%. In addition, the cost of living in
France has increased 1.6% over the past year.

James, a record company owner returning home with his family after a three-night break in France, said, 'Next year we are going to Italy. I think it is 20% cheaper there.'

France, Britain's favourite holiday destination, has had a tough year. Recent terrorist scares capped a summer when the sterling exchange rate dropped as low as 7.2 francs, very hot weather kept Britons at home, and a holiday price war cut package prices to Greece. Another price war among ferries has helped the French market, boosting last minute bookings and the day trip market. The opening of the Channel Tunnel has been an added incentive. But most families plan around school holidays, often booking a year in advance and hoping the days of Fr10 to the pound might return. They haven't.

The full impact of the currency rate on many French businesses has been severe. However, French supermarkets have done well as families buy their own food and avoid restaurants. The French Government's Tourist Office believes that it can match last year's figure of 5.5 million Britons taking a holiday. But the experience of families abroad this year may affect holiday bookings in 1996.

1. How is the current account of the UK balance of payments affected by British holiday-makers going to France? [2 marks]
2. Using economic analysis, explain how the market for holidays in France by British tourists might be affected by each of the following:
   (a) an increase in VAT in France; [4 marks]
   (b) a change in the level of the pound sterling relative to the French franc; [4 marks]
   (c) the availability of cheaper holidays in Greece and Italy.
   [4 marks]
3. With reference to the passage, explain why the demand for holidays in France is likely to be more price elastic in the long run than in the short run. [4 marks]
4. Examine the economic consequences of the opening of the Channel Tunnel for: (a) holiday-makers; (b) employment in Britain.
   [3, 4 marks]

Chapter Four
The Common Agricultural Policy

A market-rigging monument to economic folly

This chapter examines the policy developed in the original EEC of Six countries and its subsequent modifications.

When the EEC began in 1958, about 20 per cent of its population was employed in agriculture, making this by far the largest industry. Each member state had its own agricultural policy. Harmonizing these policies was essential, otherwise they would result in different food prices in different countries, and this would distort competition – because wages are influenced by food prices.

The need to develop a common agricultural policy is stated in Article 3 of the Treaty of Rome. It is the first common policy mentioned, underlining the importance attached to it. The need to unify existing disparate national policies is obvious, but why were agricultural policies needed anyway?

Reasons for agricultural policies
Returning to medieval times, most of the population were occupied by agriculture. The process of economic development involves the transfer of much of this labour force to other activities. Necessarily, the first requirement is for an increase in *labour productivity* in agriculture, so that some labour can be released. In practice, *land productivity* increased along with that of labour, as food production increased; growing output meant declining food prices. Consequently the returns to agricultural resources in general declined. So resources were reallocated from agriculture to more profitable uses.

History demonstrates that labour is persuaded to leave agriculture only slowly, resulting in incomes that are persistently below those of other occupations. In the twentieth century, low incomes for such a large sector of the economy came to be considered as *inequitable*, and so became the focus for government intervention. The low incomes are caused by economic forces, but policies to raise them are social not economic, although there are significant economic consequences.

An economic reason for intervention is that agricultural prices are inherently *unstable* in a free market. **Price elasticities** of demand for food products are low – because consumption of food means physical consumption, and once people are full a reduction in prices will not persuade them to eat much more. Neither will a rise in price greatly reduce their desire to eat.

Imagine that the price elasticity of demand for potatoes is – 0.1, and in a particular year the yield of potatoes is low owing to drought and marketed output is reduced by 5 per cent. Clearly potato prices will rise and farmers can do nothing about it; extra potatoes can be produced only next year (i.e. the supply is perfectly inelastic in the short run). How much will prices rise? – with these data, 50 per cent!

Thus, if the price elasticity of demand is low, which it is for most agricultural products, small changes in outputs cause relatively large changes in prices. Such unstable prices fail to tell producers what consumers really want. Some action to stabilize prices is therefore likely to result in an improvement in **economic efficiency**.

There is also a *strategic argument* for intervention. A secure food supply is an essential element of policy for any government and is neglected at a country's peril. The UK discovered this in the early years of this century. Comparative advantage had been followed resulting in the UK exporting manufactures and importing food – a sound economic policy which seemed safe as there had been peace in Europe for a hundred years. When the First World War began three-quarters of the flour in British bread was imported!

The Common Agricultural Policy

The aims of the policy as stated in Article 39 may be summarized as follows:

- to increase productivity
- to raise farm incomes
- to stabilize markets
- to assure the availability of supplies
- to ensure reasonable prices for consumers.

Although the Treaty of Rome does not make it clear, the fundamental objective is the raising of farm incomes, and we now turn to the methods of achieving this – raising product prices and encouraging structural change.

Price support

The EEC decided that farmers' incomes were too low because their product prices were too low, and so it designed a policy to raise prices.

Figure 2 relates to the situation in the 1960s when the policy was introduced. The supply and demand curves relate to EEC farmers and consumers. Free trade would result in a European price level of WP,

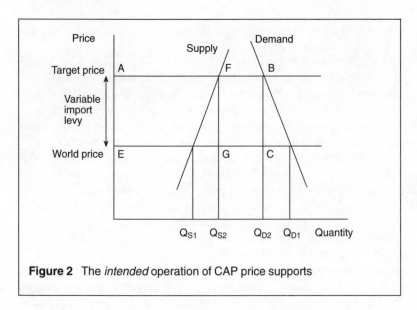

Figure 2 The *intended* operation of CAP price supports

standing for world price on the diagram. At this price, Q_{S1} and Q_{D1} would be produced and consumed respectively, the difference being imported. The EEC decided to raise the wholesale price to TP (**target price**). At this price farmers expand production to Q_{S2} and consumption declines to Q_{D2}. Cheap imports are prevented from undermining the target price by a **variable import levy** (VIL) which raises WP to at least TP.

The effects of the policy are to raise prices substantially – TP is much higher than WP – for the benefit of farmers. Prices are also stabilized, for if WP varies, the variable import levy is altered to compensate, thus keeping TP virtually constant. Consumers are worse off since they have to pay higher prices for less consumption; indeed the area ABCE (price difference times consumption) is an **implicit food tax**. Area FBCG (variable import levy times quantity imported) represents the revenue collected on imports which reduces the need for other taxation. The policy evidently transfers income from food consumers to farmers and taxpayers. Of course countries supplying imports are worse off as their market is diminished.

This support policy ignored time and the changes which it brings. Although the internal demand for food changed very little, since the population remained almost constant, supplies continually expanded under the spur of technological progress, encouraged by the artificially high level of prices.

So in Figure 3 the supply curve has moved to the right; and at the administered price TP, production exceeds consumption even in the

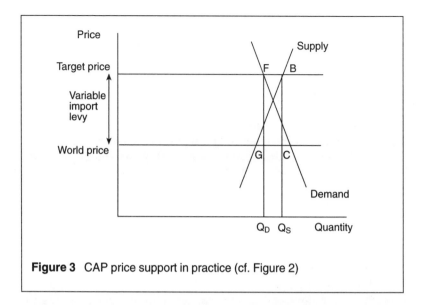

Figure 3 CAP price support in practice (cf. Figure 2)

absence of imports. Originally the policy raised prices by reducing imports; when imports have been reduced to zero as in this figure, what is to stop price falling below TP to the level indicated by the intersection of demand and supply? – an **intervention system**.

It was realized from the beginning that, for many products, a post-harvest glut would force market prices below TP even without imports. An intervention agency in each member state was formed to buy and store produce at intervention prices – set a little below target prices. Later in the season there would be *seasonal shortages*, permitting the sale of the post-harvest surpluses.

But the situation in Figure 3 became the rule: supplies increased so much that surpluses were 'normal' instead of seasonal, and they were purchased and stored with little likelihood of future release on to the internal market. These surpluses became known popularly as butter, beef and cereals *mountains* and wine *lakes*. Other products were also in surplus: there have been vegetable oil lakes and dried currant mountains for example.

Comparing Figures 2 and 3, the major change is from net imports to surpluses. What became of the latter?

Most surpluses were exported. To make this possible **export subsidies** were provided equal to TP minus WP, enabling traders to sell in world markets at world prices. Clearly this still involved a transfer of income from consumers to farmers, but now taxpayers had to pay for the removal of surpluses. Such '**dumping**' (i.e. selling abroad below cost) of Community surpluses disadvantaged third countries supplying food to the world market. On the other hand many food importers got marvellous bargains.

It should be noted that this price policy did nothing to make farming competitive in world terms. Indeed it accepted that European farming is uncompetitive and protected farmers from competition, which ensured that they never would become competitive. The difference in price levels between the internal and world markets became so large that fraud became widespread, and reputably the source of much income for the Mafia and the IRA!

Structural policy

Why was and is European agriculture uncompetitive? History bequeathed to Europe a very large number of farms, most being far too small to provide a reasonable income: small farms have high unit costs and produce little revenue. A farm can expand to become a profitable business only by increasing its land area, and as the supply of land is fixed it follows that an efficient agricultural industry means far fewer farms and *farmers*.

Here is the problem: there were, and are, millions of farmers, most of whom would. need to leave the land before agriculture could become efficient. But agricultural labour mobility is notoriously low, and as farmers die or retire too many are replaced by a new generation.

Since the 1960s, to increase mobility, there have been measures for retraining farmers for other occupations or to help them to retire. But few wish to leave agriculture and too little money has been provided for this **structural policy** to have much impact. Enthusiasm for such policies was notably lacking in the early days of the EEC when the economies of the Six were expanding rapidly. The widespread unemployment of more recent years has made any restructuring of farming far more difficult. Quite simply, there have been no jobs for ex-farmers to go to; *they might as well farm inefficiently as become unemployed.*

Green currencies

The price support policy was completed in 1968 – that is, agricultural prices in the member states had been gradually changed until they reached common levels. But then, events conspired to upset these common prices.

A world system of fixed exchange rates had operated successfully for about 24 years, now it began to break up. The common prices for agricultural products were denominated in units of account (now

European Currency Units, or Ecus) which translated into member states' currencies at fixed rates. In 1969 the French franc was devalued and the German mark revalued. At the new currency values, *since agricultural prices were in units of account*, the prices of French agricultural products should have increased (there are now more francs per unit of account) whilst German prices should have fallen.

Neither country was willing to permit these price changes, the French saying that higher food prices were inflationary and the Germans that lower prices would reduce farmers' incomes unacceptably. So although all other industries had to put up with the consequences of the currency changes, the out-of-date currency values were retained in both countries just for agriculture; i.e. prices in France were lower and in Germany higher than the agreed common prices.

To prevent these price differences distorting trade in agricultural products, a system of border taxes and subsidies was introduced. These **monetary compensatory amounts** (MCAs) became increasingly important as currency changes became more frequent. As they permitted the use of artificial exchange rates for internal agricultural trade, these rates became known as **green currencies**.

It is ironic that in a common market, the size of the MCAs became so large that real price differences for agricultural products often exceeded those existing between member states before the EEC began. *This is clearly a serious distortion of competition – such price differences prevent the operation of comparative advantage.* MCAs have been removed under the Single Market programme: if green currencies diverge by more than 5 per cent they must be revalued or devalued. But member states can compensate their farmers for these changes, with 50 per cent of the cost being met by the EU. Clearly this is a move towards common prices.

Consequences of the CAP

Have its policy objectives been achieved? Certainly productivity has increased, and supplies have been assured, both partly the result of high prices. The manipulated price system has also stabilized prices. What is 'reasonable' cannot be objectively defined, so it is a matter of opinion whether or not prices to consumers have been reasonable.

What is beyond doubt is that the primary objective of raising farm incomes to levels comparable to those of other sectors has not been achieved. Before the inception of the CAP, and today, farmers on average have incomes about half of those of the non-farming members of society; the policy has completely failed to improve their relative position.

Averages always hide much information. In the present case consider who benefits most from higher prices – clearly the farmers who produce most. These large farmers also have lower unit production costs (economies of size). *So the CAP has been helping the larger, relatively wealthy farmers, whilst leaving the poorer small farmers still poor.* Also, the policy has transferred income from consumers to producers, including transfers from poor consumers – for even the poor must eat – to richer farmers! On equity grounds such income transfers have few supporters.

Fields that grow nothing yield lucrative harvest

FOR the past five years, Robert Sherriff and his wife Penny have been paid £27,000 a year for growing only grass on more than half their 600-acre farm. They will be paid as much as £42,000 this year.

Mr Sherriff is one of 35,000 arable farmers in Britain expected to apply for grants of up to £129 for every acre on which they do not plant crops. About 1.7 million acres, bigger than Lincolnshire, could be left fallow at a cost to the taxpayer of £200 million.

Faced with mounting food surpluses, Britain and other European Community states are paying farmers to grow nothing to counter years of paying them subsidies to grow too much.

The Sherriffs started harvesting cash rather than crops at Bayford, Hertfordshire, in 1988, when they volunteered with a few other pioneers for a five-year trial of the set-aside scheme. Since last year, set-aside has become virtually compulsory for arable farmers with more than 40 acres.

'I was attracted by the security of income,' Mr Sherriff said. 'There was a lot of talk in 1988 of agricultural reform and even of doing away with price support. Setaside offered a guaranteed £88 an acre for doing nothing except mow the grass once a year. About 150 acres of the farm had always been marginal, low-yielding land anyway.'

Mr Sherriff put down to grass 300 acres that had previously grown wheat, beans and oilseed rape. With half the farm idle, he laid off the two farmhands he had employed and hires contractors for such work as ploughing and spraying. Economists believe that at least one farming job is lost for every 300 acres set aside.

This year, under the even more generous compulsory scheme, Mr Sherriff is thinking of setting aside up to 375 acres. He will be entitled to £129 an acre for 60 per cent of this fallow area and £88 an acre for the rest, a total of about £42,000.

By taking part of his land out of production, he will qualify for other grants on the crops he does grow: £77 for each of his 170 acres of wheat and £144 for each of his 55 acres of beans, a further £21,000. The money is guaranteed even if his crops fail.

The Times, 21 March 1994

There are two other major areas affected by the CAP which must be considered: the financial and economic consequences.

• Financial consequences

The financial consequences arise from the need to dispose of the surpluses generated by the high-price system. These financial costs are met by the **Agricultural Guarantee and Guidance Fund** (usually known by the acronym FEOGA from its title in French) which has consistently dominated the budget, as shown in Table 5. So large is the expenditure on agricultural support that little has been left to finance other common policies. Consequently, the development of other policy areas has been hindered.

Table 5 Budgetary expenditure of the EU, selected years 1971–95 (million Ecus)

Year	Agricultural fund	Social fund	Regional fund	Industry energy research	Adminis-tration	Other	Totals	Agriculture's % share
1971	1884	57	—	65	132	152	2289	82
1975	4587	360	150	99	375	643	6214	74
1979	10736	596	672	288	864	1448	14603	74
1983	16331	801	2266	1216	1162	2990	24766	66
1987	23939	2542	2562	965	1740	3721	35469	67
1991	33443	3869	5180	1919	2519	9656	56586	59
1992	38462	4817	7579	2424	2927	6619	62828	61
1993	37135	5907	8172	2834	3296	9705	66240	56
1994	40751	6240	8649	3194	3618	7562	70014	58
1995	40247	6498	10531	3295	3691	7695	71955	56

Source: *European Economy 62,* 1996.

• Economic efficiency

The economic consequences of the CAP are of two types – conventional and environmental.

In terms of *conventional* economics, the fact that agriculture is much more heavily protected/subsidized than other industries means that it uses some resources which could be used more profitably elsewhere. Thus on the grounds of efficiency there is significant **resource misallocation** within the EU. As the other industrialized countries outside the EU have their own agricultural support systems, some even more protective than the CAP, the misallocation is of global significance.

The protection of agriculture is believed to contribute to unemployment in EU manufacturing. It is argued that because the CAP expands

EU agricultural production to the point of major dumping on world markets (the EU is the world's second largest exporter of agricultural products), it must make countries which have a comparative advantage in agricultural production poorer. As a result their imports of manufactures from the EU are reduced, and it follows that so is employment in manufacturing industry. This problem is compounded by high food prices in the EU which help to raise costs via wages in other industries and damage their international competitiveness.

Green economics

Some of the environmental side-effects of the CAP merit a mention in passing. The CAP has encouraged, through its high prices, the ploughing of chalk downs in the south of England, and moors in the north, which at world prices would have remained as grazing lands. Wild flowers, butterflies and many other insects, bird and mammal populations have been much reduced. Putting a monetary value on environmental amenities is notoriously difficult – how would you value a beautiful view, or a colony of rare wild flowers?

Public attention tends to concentrate on the damage caused by the CAP, but it has its positive side too. Without the CAP's subsidization of livestock production in the remote and unprofitable regions of the EU – which account for huge areas of mountains, hills and moors etc. – agriculture would have disappeared from these regions. The loss of grazing animals would have resulted in the replacement of pleasant alpine meadows, for example, by bracken and scrub; depopulation and a collapse of the infrastructure would have made tourism in such regions a thing of the past.

CAP reform

The failure of the CAP to provide 'fair' incomes for the small farmers despite its vast cost has led to the universal recognition that reform is necessary. *Unfortunately the true economic costs are difficult to quantify and seem to make little impact on politicians; they therefore base their decisions almost entirely upon the financial costs although these are of secondary importance.* So reforms are aimed at reducing the budgetary costs without addressing the other ill effects of the policy.

The undesirable consequences of the CAP largely result from high prices, but reducing them significantly is regarded as politically unacceptable and politicians therefore sought other ways of reducing budgetary costs. In 1984 a **quota system** was introduced for milk. This limits the support for milk production to a predetermined quota output, with extra production attracting a much lower price. This reduces the surpluses which must be disposed of (as butter) and hence the costs. However, it still leaves the consumers paying high prices and supporting producers via an implicit food tax.

The box below outlines the latest reform packages. The **MacSharry Plan** was conceived under the intense pressure of the Uruguay round of GATT trade negotiations. Initially the proposed reforms were too little

---

The MacSharry reforms

'Major reforms', which turned out to be little more than tinkering, were agreed in 1988. The reforms introduced the quota principle to some of the major crops as a **stabilizer system**. This sought to stabilize outputs and financial costs by reducing the prices of outputs which exceeded set thresholds (notice how words like 'stabilize' and 'threshold' were used instead of politically less acceptable words like 'limit' and 'quota'). In the event, the thresholds set were too generous and the price reductions for above-threshold production were too timid for the stabilizer system to have much impact on output or support costs.

A voluntary **'set aside'** system was also introduced. This offered a subsidy to farmers who agreed to take some of their land out of production, thus reducing output. The rewards offered were too low to be attractive to farmers, so again the impact on output was negligible.

Agricultural Commissioner Ray MacSharry made much more radical reform proposals in 1991. After months of heated debate a modified version was adopted by the Council of Ministers in 1992.

The pivotal change was a phased reduction in cereal prices to bring them 'close' to world prices by 1997, with compensatory **direct income payments** being paid to farmers (approximately the price reduction times the average yield in the locality times the number of hectares grown). To receive compensatory payments a farmer had to agree to set aside at least 15 per cent of the farm's arable area. Set-aside land attracted a payment approximately equal to the profit foregone. Lower cereal prices imply reduced costs of animal feeds and the plan therefore included cuts in the prices of livestock products. (Except milk, for which the quota system is retained.)

The plan is remarkable because it attempts to replace politically manipulated prices with prices near to world market levels.

for the USA and too much for the French. After protracted and often heated US–EU negotiations an eventual compromise gave a new GATT agreement on 15 December 1993, almost three years beyond the original deadline and eight years after the negotiations began.

The economic effects of the CAP reforms include lower food prices for consumers. This is a radical change because it transfers support costs from consumers to taxpayers. Lower agricultural prices and outputs will permit a more rational allocation of resources within the EU. The international allocation of resources will also be ameliorated by a reduction in the quantity of EU surpluses being dumped on the world market.

The redistributive effects of the reformed CAP will also be more equitable in that poor consumers will no longer have to pay such high food prices to support farmers. However, the benefits to farmers will still accrue largely to the richer farmers. In 1991 MacSharry proposed a ceiling on individual farmer receipts of the direct income payments which his plan was to introduce. The UK government complained that such an arrangement would discriminate against its larger and more efficient farmers – it did not publicly comment that such farmers were also amongst the more wealthy or that they usually voted for the current government. *Thus the UK persuaded the EU to miss an opportunity to achieve a more equitable distribution of incomes within farming.*

Conclusion

Until the early 1990s the EU avoided any significant reform of the CAP despite its obvious market-rigging folly, its vast expense and its failure to achieve its main income objective. However, the importance of trade to the EU turned out to be the lever which forced reform in the context of the Uruguay Round of GATT trade negotiations. Although output should in future be more subject to market forces, resource returns to land and farmers will still be heavily subsidized, and the distribution of the gains within farming will still be mainly to the richer farmers. The Commission acknowledges the need for further reform, particularly in the context of the accession of eastern European countries (see Chapter 8), where application of the currrent CAP would enormously increase its budgetary burden.

KEY WORDS

Price elasticities
Economic efficiency
Price support
Target price
Variable import levy
Implicit food tax
Intervention system
Export subsidies
Dumping
Structural policy
European Currency Units

Monetary compensatory
   amounts
Green currencies
Agricultural Guarantee and
   Guidance Fund
Resource misallocation
Quota system
MacSharry Plan
Stabilizer system
Set aside
Direct income payments

Essay topics

1. (a) Explain the objectives of the EU's Common Agricultural Policy
   (CAP). [10 marks]
   (b) Comment on the extent to which there is a misallocation of
   resources as a consequence of the CAP. [10 marks]
   [University of Cambridge Local Examinations Syndicate 1997]

2. (a) Under the EU's set-aside programme, farmers are paid *not* to
   grow food. What justification could be offered for this policy?
   [40 marks]
   (b) Examine the likely economic effects of a decision by the EU to
   abandon the Common Agricultural Policy. [60 marks]
   [University of London Examinations and Assessment Council
   1997]

Data response question

The following task is based on a question set by the University of
London Examinations and Assessment Council in 1996. Read the arti-
cle 'Jobless Europe', which is reproduced from *The Economist* of 26
June 1993. Then answer the questions.

Jobless Europe

Business is booming for suppliers of bad ideas on how to cut unemployment. A careful appraisal of which anti-unemployment measures to adopt, and which to avoid, is still needed. In the present debate, there are three main groups: those who argue that the European Union's unemployment is cyclical, implying that the cure is to ease monetary policy; those who see the problem as mainly structural, and conclude that improved competitiveness by itself is the cure; and those who agree that the unemployment is structural, but would rather raise import barriers against suppliers in Eastern Europe and developing countries.

All three groups are dangerously in error. For a start, Europe's unemployment is plainly neither cyclical nor structural, but a mixture of both. Its cyclical part is largely due to Germany, whose policies have obliged other members of the ERM to keep interest rates higher than they would wish.

Those who are keen on faster growth think monetary policy is, therefore, too tight. But unemployment in the EU has averaged 9.9% of the labour force for the past ten years; even at the most recent peak in economic activity the rate was 9.3%. Given such figures, it is clear that a large part of the EU's unemployment problem is deep-seated and non-cyclical. Something more imaginative than pumping up aggregate demand is needed to deal with it.

What exactly? Improved competitiveness, desirable as that is, will not be enough. Low unemployment requires a flexible market for labour. Often, that goes hand in hand with greater competitiveness, and policies to further the one will tend to help the other. You also need a labour market that works, one that moves workers displaced from contracting industries into new jobs in expanding ones.

A chief cause – especially of the rising toll of long-term unemployment – is welfare benefits that are too generous for too long, and which place too few demands on recipients to find a new job.

A government must avoid doing things that make unemployment worse. There is little doubt, for instance, that France's high rate of unemployment among the young is partly due to the national minimum wage – at nearly 50% of average earnings (covering roughly 12% of wage-earners).

Greater competitiveness (unlike new trade barriers) would make the EU richer. Policies to foster it are certainly desirable. But on their own they will not cure Europe's unemployment sickness.

1. What is the distinction between structural and cyclical unemployment? [2 marks]
2. Why has Germany played a key role in European interest rate determination? [3 marks]
3. What is meant by a 'flexible market for labour'? [2 marks]
4. Explain, with the aid of a diagram, the argument that 'France's high rate of unemployment among the young is partly due to the national minimum wage at nearly 50% of average earnings'. [4 marks]
5. Other than the policies mentioned in the passage, what supply side measures could governments use to reduce the level of unemployment? [5 marks]
6. What might be the economic impact of 'raising import barriers against suppliers in Eastern Europe and developing countries'? [4 marks]

Chapter Five

Regional policy

The exploitation of comparative advantage may result in a regionally inequitable distribution of gains.

Chapters 2 and 3 dealt with the economic gains which were to flow from the introduction of free trade within Europe, both theoretically and in practice, particularly via the single market. Free trade permits efficiency and the maximization of total income within the Union, but what about the distribution of that income? The effects on various groups – local, regional or national – may exacerbate existing inequalities. This chapter considers why the gains from the exploitation of comparative advantage may be distributed inequitably, and the consequent need for redistributive intervention. Regional policy should be seen as the first explicitly redistributive aspect of the EU. We now turn to the nature and causes of regional problems and the common policies designed to ameliorate them.

The nature and causes of regional problems

The major features of regional problems are relatively low incomes, low productivity and high unemployment. Clearly these are interrelated. They are caused by a variety of **market imperfections**.

- Firstly, in the real world perfect mobility of factors or products does not exist. So locational factors become very important. These include access to large markets, access to inputs (raw materials, centres of administrative or financial expertise), access to skilled labour.
- Secondly, comparing labour markets in different regions, wage differentials sometimes exceed productivity differences. Thus 'efficiency wages' – wages divided by productivity – can vary considerably, effectively rendering some regions uncompetitive.
- Thirdly, labour is not perfectly mobile. In practice the least skilled labour is least mobile. Conversely, the most skilled labour generally is mobile and leaves poor regions for employment in richer regions. These differences in labour mobilities exacerbate any initial regional income disparity.

A region may become depressed through some autonomous change in demand or supply or the interplay of market forces. In the EU context, comparative advantage benefits the more efficient firms which expand their outputs and supplant the less efficient firms. Expansion and contraction are opposite sides of the same coin. Because of the market imperfections noted above, the gainers and losers from the Single Market tend to be regionally concentrated. A depressed region is unattractive to entrepreneurs and therefore lacks investment, so the depression becomes cumulative.

There is no reason to expect market forces to correct regional imbalances. Regional income disparities are thus a form of **market failure** and government intervention is essential to their amelioration.

When one country becomes depressed relative to others with which it trades it is able to restore its competitiveness by depreciating its currency. Regions within a country are unable to help themselves to adjust in this fashion because they belong to a single currency nation. In future, when the Union becomes a single currency group of nations each will have lost the exchange rate method of overcoming a loss of competitiveness. Evidently, a future EMU will make regional policy extremely important.

In the 1990s, national income disparities are substantial. International comparisons of living standards are fraught with difficulty but comparisons of GDP per head in terms of '**purchasing power standards**' give a reasonably fair indication. On this basis the eight richest members of the Union are reasonably close together, enjoying incomes significantly higher than those of the poorer four. In Greece and Portugal, GDP per head is about half that of the average of the eight. In Ireland and Spain, GDPs per head are about two-thirds and three-quarters respectively of the average of the eight. The poorest regions of the poorer countries have average incomes which are only a quarter of those of the richest regions of the richer countries.

There are two main types of depressed region:

- *Rural areas* where there is a heavy dependence upon agriculture, particularly if the farms are small leading to low labour productivity. Such areas are characterized by high unemployment and poorly developed infrastructures. The main low-income agricultural regions are the south of Italy, most of Greece, Ireland, Portugal and large areas of Spain.
- *Urban areas* where traditional industries, such as coal mining, steel production, and shipbuilding are declining. The depressed urban regions typically suffer high unemployment, decaying housing and infrastructures, and social deprivation. They are found largely in Belgium, France, the eastern part of the unified Germany and the UK.

The evolution of regional policy

When the Union began in 1958 the original six members had their own different regional policies. Such national policies were generally intended to assist 'backward' regions, such as areas where traditional industries were in decline, to catch up with other areas. But at what level does assistance cease merely to compensate for regional disadvantages and become unfair national aids which distort competition? Clearly some Union-level policy coordination was necessary if competitive forces were not to be negated. But in practice, so long as the Union enjoyed rapid economic growth and high overall employment, these issues were left to member states. Common policy was restricted to the establishment of the **European Investment Bank** (EIB). This was called for by Article 3 of the Treaty of Rome, largely with the south of Italy – the Mezzogiorno – in mind as the only major relatively poor area in the original Six countries.

The same Article called for the establishment of a **European Social Fund** (some aspects of social policy are discussed in Chapter 3). The ESF dealt with employment issues, particularly the retraining of workers displaced by structural change, leaving the main areas of social policy such as health, education, housing and pensions, to national authorities. EIB expenditures were, and still are, concentrated on improvements to infrastructures (improved roads, water supplies etc.) in the poorer regions. The complementary nature of the expenditures of the ESF in these regions to improve working conditions and provide training – in short to raise labour productivity – makes the Social Fund a part of regional policy.

In the early days of the CAP, its price supporting activities were also thought of as having a regional role, in raising incomes in poor agricultural regions. As discussed in Chapter 4, the CAP tended in practice to favour the richer farmers in the richer regions, and its price-distorting activities have been of little benefit in reducing regional income disparities. However, the Guidance Section of FEOGA does have a regional role and its assistance has been focused on the poorer agricultural regions. Guidance Section expenditure is now considered to be part of the regional structural funds.

The coincidence of EU enlargement problems, a reduction in the rate of economic growth and global depression in the mid 1970s increased general unemployment and left few opportunities for unemployed workers in poorer areas. Regional problems were thus highlighted, resulting in the establishment of the **European Regional Development Fund** (ERDF) in 1975. This was particularly welcomed by the UK which saw a regional policy as a means of obtaining some redistributive benefits to help in offsetting the large budgetary transfers resulting from CAP arrangements; between 1975 and 1992 the UK received just over £4 billion from the ERDF which, although helping to offset CAP transfers, still left the UK as a major net contributor to the EU budget.

The UK continues to need, and to receive, large quantites of aid for its declining areas, as reported in the article from *The Times*. ERDF contributes towards matching national expenditures to stimulate the economic development or reconstruction of poorer regions.

The accession of Greece in 1981 and Portugal and Spain in 1986, all relatively poor countries, increased the importance of regional policies and EU expenditures increased substantially as shown in Table 6.

At the same time the Single European Act envisaged the introduction of the Single Market which might increase existing regional disparities. Accordingly the SEA formally recognized the importance of regional redistribution and called for the coordination of existing policies and

Biggest EC hand-out goes to Britain

Britain continues to suffer the worst industrial decline in the European Community, the European Commission indicated yesterday.

The Commission announced areas that will qualify for aid in the next three years. Britain's total of £1.69 billion is the highest in the Community. To qualify for aid, areas must have higher general and industrial unemployment rates than the EC averages.

Parts of London were designated areas of industrial decline for the first time for having some of the worst unemployment blackspots. Most of Scotland will gain, as will Tyne and Wear, Humberside, parts of the West Midlands and Gibraltar. Some aid goes to Durham, Greater Manchester, South Yorkshire, Cheshire and Cumbria.

Parts of the London boroughs of Enfield, Hackney, Haringey, Newham, Tower Hamlets and Waltham Forest will receive aid for the first time, as well as Thanet in Kent.

'It's very good news for London,' Bruce Millan, EC regional affairs commissioner said. 'For the first time it has been recognised by the Community that London has major problems'.

However, the Government said yesterday that it was 'disappointed' by the commission's aid allocation. Tim Sainsbury, the Industry Minister, said the allocation 'does not fully reflect' Britain's problems.

'We pressed the Commission to recognise the justification for a much greater coverage of urban areas,' he said. The Government is particularly concerned that large swaths of London and the East Thames corridor missed out, as well as Bristol, Derby and Leicester.

Although Britain's £1.69 billion is slightly less than in the last spending round four years ago, it is still more than any other EC country's allocation.

The Times, 22 December 1993

Table 6 Expenditures of the regional policy funds, selected years 1975–95 (million Ecus)

	European Investment Bank	European Regional Development fund	European Social fund
1975	814	150	360
1980	2384	752	502
1985	5699	1624	1413
1990	10996	4554	3212
1991	13672	5180	3869
1992	12974	7579	4817
1993	14224	8172	5097
1994	14148	8649	6240
1995	12395	10531	6498

Source: *European Economy 62,* 1996.

increased funding. The ERDF, ESF and the Guidance Section of FEOGA were grouped together as the **structural funds** whose activities were to be coordinated.

How does regional policy work?
At the beginning of this chapter the major problems were diagnosed as being poor location with respect to markets (i.e. high transport costs) and low labour productivity. It is at these two characteristics that expenditures have been targeted. The ESF focuses on retraining workers to raise their productivity, EIB loans and ERDF grants concentrate on improvements to transport infrastructures. Such expenditures have been largely in the poorer regions of the poorer member countries. *The thrust of the policy is to improve the economic environments of poor regions so that investment is attracted into them.*

The expanding importance of regional policy
In 1988 the European Council decided to double in real terms the resources devoted to structural funds over the next five years, and to give priority to regions where GDP per head was less than 75 per cent of the EU average.

The TEU expanded the policy further, creating a **Committee of Regions** and a **Cohesion Fund.** The latter is to help countries where the GNP is less than 90 per cent of the EU average – Greece, Ireland, Portugal and Spain – to meet the 'convergence criteria'; thus there is an explicit link to 'economic and monetary union' (EMU). When the latter removes monetary and exchange rate policies from national governments, whole member states, unable to adjust to changing economic circumstances, could become 'poorer regions'. Regional policy will then become one of several redistributive policies required to compensate for the inequitable distribution of incomes which the free market will generate.

From 1993 another major increase in resources began, with the structural and cohesion funds set to reach 35 per cent of total EU expenditure by 1999.

Conclusion

Regional policy has its origins in the need to assist the poorer regions, both rural areas heavily dependent on small farms and urban areas with a concentration of declining industries. *As European integration proceeds, the gains from the exploitation of comparative advantage tend to benefit some regions more than others – indeed the decline of some areas may be accelerated.* Consequently, redistributive regional policies are increasingly important; by1992 such structural policies already accounted for a quarter of the EU budget, and they are to increase to 35 per cent by 1999. The poorer EU regions and states are benefiting from a substantial transfer of resources. The further integration represented by economic and monetary union, examined in the next chapter, together with further enlargements discussed in Chapter 8, will greatly expand the role of regional and other redistributive policies.

KEY WORDS

Market imperfections	European Regional
Market failure	Development Fund
Purchasing power	Structural funds
European Investment Bank	Committee of Regions
European Social Fund	Cohesion Fund

Essay topics

1. (a) With reference to examples of your choice, explain why the European Community developed common policies such as those for agriculture, transport, regional and social affairs. {12 marks]
   (b) Are these likely to become more or less important as a consequence of the Single European Market? Justify your answer.

[8 marks]

[University of Cambridge Local Examinations Syndicate 1996]

2. (a) How is the performance of an economy affected by *both* the geographical *and* the occupational mobility of labour? [12 marks]
   (b) Outline the various ways in which the government can seek to improve the mobility of labour, and examine critically the arguments for and against such intervention by the government.

[13 marks]

[Associated Examining Board 1996]

Data response question

The following task is based on a question set by the University of Cambridge Local Examinations Syndicate in 1995. Read the article and study the map (adapted from *The Guardian*, 25 May 1993). Then answer all the questions.

NORTH FIGHTS BACK IN SWAN'S CRISIS

The entrance to the Swan Hunter Shipyard on Tyneside has a steep slope, like a slipway. On Friday, 420 of the 2000 workers will walk down that slipway for the last time. There remains harrowing uncertainty for the remainder of one of the highest skilled manufacturing workforces in Europe.

The crisis at Swan Hunter focuses a piercing spotlight on government policy on manufacturing and sets a question mark against the stated commitment to intervention of the President of the Board of Trade, Michael Heseltine. Swan's went into receivership twelve days ago after losing a £170 m helicopter carrier order to a partnership led by VSEL, based in Barrow-in-Furness (also in the North). The threat to Swan is an indication of the radical nature of structural employment changes faced by this struggling region.

The number of jobs in Tyne and Wear is expected to rise by only 5600 (1.2%) by 2001. Sweeping changes will see an expansion in part-time, service sector and female employment as manufacturing, the region's historic bedrock, which has provided full-time jobs for men, shrinks. Forecasts suggest that the manufacturing workforce will decline by 25%, leaving it as only 15.5% of the total by 2001. Full-time employment is projected to fall by 24%; self-employment is expected to grow by 15%.

Investment by Japanese firms such as car manufacturing giant Nissan have brought new opportunities, but also potential dangers to the region. Nissan symbolizes the revival of manufacturing in the North-East, a region without a history of motor manufacturing. Production, though, this year has stalled and indicators suggest that the flow of inward Japanese investment is likely to diminish. The North-East has enjoyed less inward investment in the 1980s while, in contrast, Portugal has seen a forty-fold increase in investment from Japanese companies.

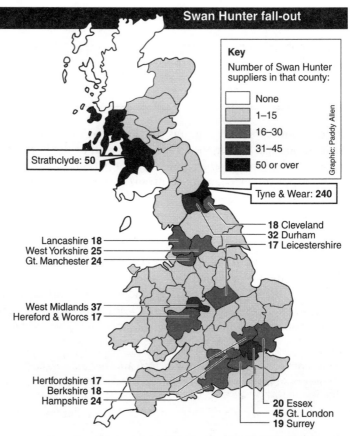

Swan Hunter fall-out

Key
Number of Swan Hunter suppliers in that county:

- None
- 1–15
- 16–30
- 31–45
- 50 or over

Graphic: Paddy Allen

Strathclyde: **50**

Tyne & Wear: **240**

18 Cleveland
32 Durham
17 Leicestershire

Lancashire **18**
West Yorkshire **25**
Gt. Manchester **24**

West Midlands **37**
Hereford & Worcs **17**

Hertfordshire **17**
Berkshire **18**
Hampshire **24**

20 Essex
45 Gt. London
19 Surrey

© M. Halsall, *North Fights Back in Swan Crisis*, adapted from *The Guardian*, 25 May 1993

1. (a) State **two** indicators of deindustrialization referred to in the article. [2 marks]
   (b) Explain why these are appropriate indicators. [2 marks]
2. In July 1994, Swan Hunter went into receivership and it was unlikely that the company could continue to operate.
   With reference to the map:
   (a) How will the closure have affected Tyne and Wear? [2 marks]
   (b) Explain how the information can be applied to illustrate the multiplier process. [4 marks]
3. Use the case of Swan Hunter to explain how deindustrialization might have affected the UK's balance of payments. [4 marks]
4. Assess the costs and benefits of inward Japanese investment to a region such as Tyne and Wear which is facing deindustrialization.

[6 marks]

Chapter Six

Economic and monetary union

One market ... one money

═══════════════════════════════

Economic and monetary union is the final stage in economic integration; it alone will enable the EU to capture all of the benefits of the Single Market. It means the replacement of national currencies with a single European currency and centralized control of monetary and economic policies. *It involves such a pooling of sovereignty that political union is the only logical conclusion.*

The EMU debate

There is a limit to the degree of market integration which can be achieved so long as national currencies and economic policies exist. Even in the absence of tariff barriers, and if all technical standards and company law were harmonized and all non-tariff barriers removed, national currencies would still inhibit competition. They do this in two ways:

- The conversion of one currency into another adds to costs.
- The possibility that the exchange rates between currencies may change during a deal adds substantially to uncertainty. These uncertainties are magnified by differences in inflation rates.

Finally, different economic policies in member states result in different rates of interest and different methods and rates of taxation for both companies and consumers. It follows that the full benefits of the internal market can only be achieved by full economic and monetary union.

Brief mention should be made here of the CAP. One of its problems has been that of uncommon prices caused by the 'green' currency exchange rate system. A common currency would resolve this difficulty and ease the operation of the CAP in either its old or reformed state.

What is the economic case against EMU?

Take the case of a member country with balance of payments problems causing its exchange rate to fall. It has three policy options:

- It can use its reserves of gold and foreign currency to support its desired exchange rate.

- It can raise its interest rate to increase the international demand for its currency.
- It can cure the underlying problem. For example, it may be that a high inflation rate is making the country uncompetitive, so that anti-inflationary policies are required.

Any or all of these policies may fail and then equilibrium must be restored by altering the exchange rate, or permitting it to be determined by market forces. If the country in question is locked into an EMU, it possesses none of these options – its currency is the common currency, fixed in terms of its partners, and it has the same rate of inflation as its partners. So if its workers demand higher wages and fail to increase productivity accordingly they will become unemployed; national economic policy has no power beyond that of persuasion to help them.

In reality these arguments against EMU are political in that control over economic policy instruments is lost by individual countries. This loss of control is indeed very substantial. The possibility of one country becoming depressed relative to the others implies corrective action involving considerable resource transfers; ultimately redistributive regional policies as part of a central budget and central economic policy control would be essential.

As the EMU debate turns out to be largely political, the present discussion must avoid taking sides and will concentrate on the economic issues. These deal with how EMU may be achieved, and chart developments.

How can EMU be achieved?

There are four essential elements to EMU:

- a single currency
- an EU central bank
- an EU economic policy
- EU political control.

A single currency, the first hurdle, is the one which appears to attract most attention – not surprisingly, for once this has been agreed the other elements of EMU must follow.

The transition towards EMU would be very disruptive if economic conditions between member states differed much when a single currency was introduced. Consequently detailed **convergence criteria** have been agreed. They are set out in the Treaty on European Union ('Maastricht'), and continue the general direction of **cohesion policy** followed since EMU was called for in the Single European Act. Each member state should satisfy the criteria before joining the EMU. The criteria relate to:

- price stability
- favourable interest rates
- stable exchange rates
- a reasonable level of government debt.

Price stability is defined as an annual rate of inflation which is no more than 1.5 per cent above that of the average of the three best performing member states. A favourable interest rate is similarly defined except that the permitted maximum difference is 2 per cent. A stable exchange rate means keeping within the ERM band for at least two years. Finally, government debt must be no more than 60 per cent of GDP. We now turn to the common cooperative attempt to stabilize exchange rates.

The European Monetary System

The EMS was introduced in 1979 with two main aims: first to increase economic convergence, and second to create a zone of monetary stability within the Community to foster internal trade. Of course these aims have to be seen against the long-term aim of EMU to which they would contribute.

As part of the EMS each member state (including the UK) handed 20 per cent of its gold and foreign currency reserves to the **European Monetary Cooperation Fund** in return for Ecus. These can be used in transactions within the EU. The Ecu (**European Currency Unit**) was introduced (replacing the very similar European Unit of Account) as a composite currency; i.e. it is a unit based on a 'weighted basket' of members' currencies. The weight assigned to each currency is in proportion to the relative size of that country's economy. As Germany is the largest economy in the Community it has a large weight in the Ecu. The composition of the Ecu was reviewed every few years, but it is now fixed until the single currency is introduced, as shown in Table 7.

The **Exchange Rate Mechanism** (ERM) is the central part of the EMS and its operation is intended to provide exchange rate stability. The currency of each member has a specific value (**parity**) in terms of the Ecu. In turn this means that each currency has a parity value in terms of each of the other member currencies. When the ERM began

Table 7 Composition of the Ecu in 1996

Currency	Percentage weights
Belgian franc	7.8
Danish krone	2.5
German mark	30.5
Greek drachma	0.8
Spanish peseta	5.2
French franc	19.4
Irish punt	1.1
Italian lira	9.9
Luxembourg franc	0.3
Dutch guilder	9.5
Portugese escudo	0.8
British pound	12.1
Total	100.00

Source: *Europe in the Round* 1996–7 CD ROM.

any one currency was permitted to vary by plus or minus 2.25 per cent against any other member currency. When this margin was reached the two central banks concerned had to intervene to keep within the limits.

There was a second element to the mechanism, a **divergence indicator**, which was three-quarters of a country's permitted variation against the Ecu. When this indicator was reached the country was expected to take corrective action. Thus if the currency fell in value the government might increase interest rates, increase taxation or support the currency.

By 1989 only the three poorest southern European member states – Greece, Portugal and Spain – together with the UK, had not joined the ERM. The three intended to join as soon as their economic circumstances permitted, and Spain did so in 1989 and Portugal in 1992, both with 6 per cent permitted bands of variation against their central parity.

In the UK, political opposition to the ERM, because it was seen as yet another sacrifice of sovereignty, militated against joining. However, against the will of many on the right of the government the UK joined in October 1990.

Appraisal of the EMS

The objectives of the EMS are economic convergence and exchange rate stability, prerequisites for economic and monetary union.

Real convergence is the convergence of EU economies to the highest current EU living standards through the catching up of the poorer countries and regions. The EMS cannot directly cause this convergence but it can help to produce the stable economic environment in which real convergence can occur, helped by the cohesion policy.

Nominal convergence implies convergence towards the lowest rates of inflation, and to balance of payments and budget balances which together encourage more stable exchange rates – the ideal prelude to EMU is exchange rates which are so stable that they can be fixed, and replaced with a single currency.

Between 1979 and 1992, inflation rates gradually converged and fell, helping sustantially to stabilize exchanges rates. The latter enjoyed stability but not rigidity: over the period there were 12 realignments agreed quietly and collectively rather than with the dramas previously associated with such changes. The stability was intra-EC, so of course fluctuations of the Ecu against external currencies were not affected.

The ERM began to be considered very successful, and was joined in 1989 by Spain, in 1990 by the UK – at what was generally considered to be too high a rate, see Chapter 7 – and finally in 1992 by Portugal. The rate of inflation in Greece was too high for ERM membership and that country has never joined.

A major reason for falling inflation rates prior to 1992 was that participation in the ERM was a constraint on domestic policies. Budget deficits were less easily cured by devaluations. Capital controls and the manipulation of short-term interest rates were the traditional methods used to keep exchange rates within their set limits. However, the liberalization of capital movements under the Single Market Programme, the reunification of Germany and the decision to proceed to EMU coincided to help destabilize the system. To meet the Maastricht criteria for EMU, countries had to reduce budget deficits at a time when the Community was moving into recession. An inflationary German budget deficit caused by reunification resulted in the Bundesbank raising interest rates to relatively high levels. The deutschmark increased in value, and to keep their exchange rates within the agreed limits in a system where the Ecu was dominated by the DM, other countries were forced to raise their interest rates. EU recession and unemployment increased but interest rates were maintained. The relative overvaluation of some currencies had been such an aid to reducing inflation that governments had been reluctant to realign.

In late 1992, speculators decided that the exchange rates of some currencies were unsustainable and massive transfers of funds forced both the lira and pound out of the ERM in September. Continued speculation during the following months forced most currencies to devalue. Eventually, intense speculation resulted in the ERM bands being widened to 15 per cent in August 1993. In the accompanying boxed article from the *Independent* the ERM is pronounced 'all but dead'.

The announcement of the death of the ERM turned out to be premature. Soon, Germany began to cut its interest rates and stability began to return. The wide bands increased flexibility, making it more difficult for speculators to mount attacks and nine countries remained within the ERM. Although the wide bands are retained, these nine gradually returned to the old narrow bands in practice. In 1995 Austria joined the ERM, followed in 1996 by Finland and Italy.

Table 8 provides the inflation rate background to the changes discussed above. The 1985 and 1990 data illustrate the general reduction in inflation during the first stable period, although German inflation is seen to have increased as a result of the reunification of East and West. After the exchange rate storms of 1992–93 stability has returned, and inflation rates are again converging on their downward paths.

Speculators humiliate ERM

Currency speculators and international investors celebrated victory over the European Community yesterday, as weak currencies in the now defunct European exchange rate mechanism were savaged and Germany was angrily blamed for the system's collapse.

European politicians said Germany had failed to respect its obligations in the ERM and had triggered its death. The European Commission warned that the dismantling of the ERM and its economic consequences threatened to put countries at each others' throats and wreck the single market.

The ERM was pronounced all but dead after the meeting of finance ministers and central bank governors broke up early on Monday morning. They let all currencies apart from the German mark and Dutch guilder fluctuate by up to 15 per cent from their central rate. Economists said the widening of the bands was purely cosmetic and that Europe had re-adopted a system of floating exchange rates after 14 years in which the ERM had been the cornerstone of European economic cooperation.

The Independent, 3 August 1993

Table 8 Rates of inflation in the EU, selected years

	1985	1990	1995	1996
Belgium	5.9	3.5	1.5	2.0
Denmark	4.3	2.7	1.8	1.8
Germany	1.8	2.8	2.0	1.6
Greece	18.3	19.9	9.3	8.3
Spain	7.1	6.5	4.6	3.6
France	5.8	2.8	1.6	1.8
Ireland	5.1	2.0	2.5	2.3
Italy	9.0	5.9	5.8	4.1
Luxembourg	4.3	5.5	2.0	1.7
Netherlands	2.4	2.2	1.1	1.9
Austria	3.3	3.3	2.2	2.1
Portugal	19.4	11.6	4.2	3.1
Finland	5.6	6.0	1.1	1.0
Sweden	6.9	9.6	2.7	1.7
UK	5.3	5.5	2.6	2.7

Source: *European Economy 62,* 1996.

The EMU timetable

The European Council has adopted a **three-stage timetable.**

- Stage 1 began in July 1990. During this stage the aim was to encourage further economic convergence, price stability, and sound public finance. The cohesion policy designed to raise the economic circumstances of the poorer Union members towards those of the richer members – discussed in the previous chapter – was a major element.

- As agreed in the TEU, stage 2 began on 1 January1994 with the establishment of the **European Monetary Institute** (EMI) as the precursor of a future **European Central Bank.** The EMI aims to increase cooperation between members' central banks, to coordinate their monetary policies, to encourage the convergence of inflation and interest rates, and help to stabilize exchange rates. *These duties of the EMI could be summarized as guiding member states towards the attainment of the four convergence criteria which are fundamental to a smooth transition to EMU.*

- Stage 3 is economic and monetary union. At the Madrid European Council in 1995 the start of this stage was agreed as 1 January 1999. Then members that do meet the criteria and wish to, will proceed to full economic and monetary union, leaving the other members outside the new union until they have caught up, their position being reviewed every two years.

On 1 January 1999 the EMI will be transmuted into the European Central Bank (ECB), and the exchange rates of participating members will be irrevocably fixed in terms of the **Euro** – the new name of the Ecu. National currencies will coexist with the Euro until 2002 when only the Euro will be legal tender. The ECB will be independent of the Commission, the European Parliament and national governments. It will define and execute EU monetary policy, undertake its foreign exchange operations, hold its foreign reserves, and be the sole issuer of notes and coin.

Clearly EMU involves huge changes in sovereignty. Those against EMU describe it as an unacceptable loss of national sovereignty; those in favour consider it to be an essential pooling of sovereignty. All EU members have signed and ratified the TEU and so presumably agree both with its timetable and with its ultimate destination.

Well, most members agree. The UK ratified the Treaty despite expressing public doubts and insisted on a protocol which leaves the final decision on joining the EMU to a future government and parliament. However, the new Labour government has a radically different attitude to the previous Conservative one and seems certain to join. Denmark also had mixed feelings and agreed an opt out which is likely to leave its final decision to a national referendum.

Conclusion

These topics clearly raise both political and economic issues which must be kept apart in the mind of the economist. On the economic benefits of EMU an empirical study, *One Market, One Money*, published in November 1990 by the Commission (with the support and advice of several economists outside the Commission) produced some interesting conclusions. It expected EMU to reduce the rate of inflation, and since there would be one currency only, exchange rate transactions costs would be removed. Both of these factors would contribute to a significant reduction in uncertainty and so encourage an expansion in investment. The consequent increase in Union GDP would be of the order of 6 per cent and dynamic in nature – that is approximately equal to the expected economic benefits of the single market discussed in Chapter 2. Some of the big questions left unanswered include:

- What happens to the countries that do not join the EMU?
- What about the required centralization of fiscal policy?

KEY WORDS

Convergence criteria	Divergence indicator
Cohesion policy	Real convergence
European Monetary	Nominal convergence
Cooperation Fund	Three-stage timetable
European Currency Unit	European Monetary Institute
Exchange Rate Mechanism	European Central Bank
Parity	Euro

Essay topics

1. Assume that the UK joins a monetary union with a single European currency. Examine the likely effects of this on:

    (a) the UK's pattern of trade;   [30 marks]

    (b) EU consumers and producers;   [40 marks]

    (c) UK macroeconomic management.   [30 marks]

    [University of London Examinations and Assessment Council 1997]

2. (a) Examine the potential economic benefits to European businesses and consumers of the introduction of a single European currency. [50 marks]
(b) For what reasons might a single European currency be disadvantageous to a member country? [50 marks]
[University of London Examinations and Assessment Council 1996]

3. (a) How has manufacturing industry in the UK been affected by the country's membership of the EU? [12 marks]
(b) Discuss the possible costs and benefits for manufacturing industry if the UK decides to rejoin the Exchange Rate Mechanism.
[13 marks]

[Associated Examining Board 1995]

Data response question
The following task is based on a question set by the University of Cambridge Local Examinations Syndicate in 1996. The charts and brief discussion below are adapted from an article in *The Economist* of 30 September 1995. Study the information and then answer all the questions.

Economic and monetary union: the EU's feel bad factor?

On the surface, the economies of member states of the European Union (EU) appear to be growing out of recession; as Fig. A shows, growth is strong, exports to non-EU countries are up sharply and prospects seem to be good. So, why do European politicians feel miserable? The answer is unemployment. One in ten workers in the EU is out of a job. Only tiny Luxembourg, with just 3.9% of the workforce jobless, can feel smug. Elsewhere, the rate varies from just below 7% in Holland and Austria to a fearful 22.1% in Spain. The threat of unemployment is straining government budgets and discrediting, perhaps permanently, the promise made by politicians to achieve Economic and Monetary Union (EMU) by 1999. A programme of convergence agreed in the Maastricht Treaty sets the following targets:

- reducing public debt to a target of 60% or less of GDP
- restraining budget deficits to 3% of GDP
- keeping inflation and interest rates low
- minimising currency fluctuations.

So far, only Luxembourg and Germany have met all of these criteria.

Figure A GDP, exports and inflation

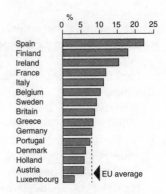

Figure B Unemployment (standardized), July 1995

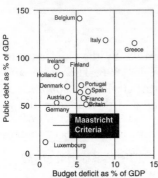

Figure C Deficits and debt, 1994

1. (a) In Figure A, the export data are shown in terms of volume rather than value. Explain the difference between these two methods of presenting export data, and suggest one reason why volume has been used in this case. [2 marks]

(b) From Figure A, comment on the relationship between export growth and GDP growth between 1990 and 1994. [2 marks]

(c) State and explain two factors, other than exports, which might have contributed to overall GDP growth in the economies of the EU. [4 marks]

2. (a) What is a budget deficit? [1 mark]

(b) Briefly state the theoretical relationship between changes in the level of unemployment and budget deficits in an economy. [2 marks]

(c) Six countries had a budget deficit of less than 5% of GDP in 1994. On the basis of the evidence provided, explain which of these six countries seems *least* likely to meet the fiscal targets set by the Maastricht Treaty. [3 marks]

3. 'There are serious obstacles to the achievement of EMU by 1999.' Use the information provided to comment upon this view. [6 marks]

Chapter Seven

Impact of membership on the UK

This royal throne of kings, this scept'red isle
This earth of majesty, this seat of Mars,
This other Eden, demi-paradise,
. . . .
With inky blots, and rotten parchment bonds;
That England, that was wont to conquer others,
Hath made a shameful conquest of itself.

John of Gaunt, in Shakespeare's *Richard II*

There are many people in the UK who see membership of the European Union as the surrender of **sovereignty** – *whether they are right or are as out of date as John of Gaunt is a matter of personal opinion.*

Political opinion in the UK remains deeply divided. Many MPs of all the major political parties are supportive of the most recent developments on European integration, but a significant number of so-called 'right-wing' politicians are very strongly opposed.

In the years leading up to 1997, deep divisions within the Conservative government led to its being – on certain issues – uncooperative with the European partners, and this soured the UK's dealings with the EU.

In November 1990 the UK's deputy prime minister resigned his post because he disagreed profoundly with Margaret Thatcher's government's approach to the whole issue. This encouraged a challenge to Mrs Thatcher for the Conservative party leadership. The ensuing election competition forced Mrs Thatcher to resign, and John Major was elected by Conservative MPs to be the new Prime Minister.

These changes in the Conservative leadership failed to heal the party divisions, which were soon exposed again in vituperous debates over the Maastricht Treaty (the TEU). The article reproduced here from *The European*, giving the views of the now Baroness Thatcher, sum up the right-wing case admirably.

Whatever his own views, Mr Major was unable to commit the UK to all of the elements of the TEU because of the influence of his right wing. Specifically, he had to refuse UK participation in the social policy (see Chapter 5), and insist that any final decision on the UK joining a future EMU must be the perogative of the government of the day. In

Baroness Thatcher says why she sees the treaty as an outdated vision of Europe

Like many of my fellow Tories, I too have a favourite quotation from Disraeli. At Manchester in 1872 he said that "the programme of the Conservative Party is to maintain the Constitution of the country". This Conservative government, like its predecessors, should have as its main priority the maintenance of our constitutional freedoms, our democratic institutions, and the accountability of Parliament to the people. Because I believe in these principles so deeply I cannot support the ratification of the Maastricht treaty, and I welcome sterling's departure from the Exchange Rate Mechanism (ERM).

The treaty will hand over more powers to unelected bureaucrats, and erode the freedoms of ordinary men and women in this country. And no mere declaration on subsidiarity is going to change the Articles or the thrust of the treaty itself – even assuming that more notice is taken of such a declaration than of those I insisted be appended to the Single European Act.

Our political debate on the Maastricht treaty and the future development of Europe has been conducted in, if possible, even less rational terms than our discussion of exchange rates. We are warned from home and abroad, that it would be a national humiliation if Britain were left in the "slow lane" while others sped towards economic and monetary union. We risk being relegated, it is delicately hinted, to the "second tier" of a two-tier Europe. We must not miss the Continental Express. We must be at the "heart" of Europe. But, as Lord Salisbury once pointed out, half the errors in politics come from taking metaphors literally.

There have been two visions of Europe competing with each other in recent years. There is, first, the federalist vision of a Europe run increasingly from Brussels, united by a common citizenship, harmonised by bureaucratic regulations, equipped with common economic, budgetary, foreign and defence policies, using a single currency and acquiring all the flags, anthems and symbols of nation-hood: all in all, a United States of Europe in embryo.

Then there is what might be called the "confederal" concept of a Europe of national states, based upon the idea of co-operation between independent sovereign countries loosely linked in a free trade area, with competition between different tax and regulatory systems and with freely floating currencies. This "confederal" Europe would accommodate the countries of eastern Europe and give them a reasonable stability. It would maintain, not jeopardise, our relationship with Europe's great friend and protector, the United States.

It is time to get our priorities right. There are more urgent things for Europe to attend to now than Maastricht. It must further free trade by completing the Uruguay round of Gatt. It must strengthen links with America, inside and outside Nato. Above all, it must use both free trade and security to help ex-communist nations build prosperity and entrench freedom.

Britain needs to regain the confidence that we can manage our own affairs successfully once more. And we need a clearly defined economic policy to encourage soundly-based growth. Maastricht can do nothing to assist but much to damage progress towards those objectives. The government must recognise that Maastricht, like the ERM, is part of the vision of yesterday. It is time to set out the vision for tomorrow.

Baroness Thatcher was British Prime Minister from 1979 to 1990.

The European, 8–11 October 1992

the event, he was unable to persuade all of his right-wing MPs to vote with the government, and so ratification of the TEU was possible only because of the support of the Liberal Democrats. Labour MPs voted against on the grounds that the UK should have accepted the whole of the Treaty rather than its mutilated remains, that is with the Social Chapter missed out and an EMU opt-out put in.

These exciting political events underline the depth of controversy that relations between the UK and EU have generated. They have been outlined here because it is essential for economists to recognize and take account of the political aspects of their analyses, but it must be emphasized that in their economic analyses *economists must remain as far as possible unbiased*. So we now turn from noting political events to asking the factual question – what is the economic impact of EU membership?

It is evident that joining has greatly reduced the policy choices available to the British government. More and more decisions are taken by the Union jointly rather than by Britain independently. Thus if the UK has a balance of payments problem, membership rules out the use of import controls or subsidies to help UK firms. Competition policy is increasingly determined in Brussels. For some years all major policy decisions affecting agriculture have been taken at Union level. *But common action can be very beneficial, the single European market could only be achieved through collective decision-making.*

The economic benefits of membership

- The UK's record

Table 9 gives some of the main economic indicators for the UK economy. It shows significant changes in the UK rate of growth since accession to the Community in 1973.

In 1974–85 the rate of economic growth was much lower than in the decade before accession. In 1986–90 economic growth resumed at the relatively high rate of 3.3 per cent. In the early 1990s the UK suffered negative growth (a contradiction in terms, but conventional usage). What factors lay behind these changes in growth rates?

The 1974–85 low-growth period was not necessarily due to any negative impact of EC membership; it is easily explained by external events. In 1974 the world price of oil increased by almost 400 per cent, followed by further significant increases at the end of the decade. This was a major factor in precipitating a worldwide depression, *so low growth rates were then the norm in all industrialized countries, although the UK was well below the EC average.*

Table 9 Evolution of the UK economy, 1961–96

	1961 to 1973	1974 to 1985	1986 to 1990	1991	1992	1993	1994	1995	1996
GDP annual real growth rate (%)	3.1	1.4	3.3	-2.0	-0.5	2.2	3.8	2.4	2.4
Gross fixed capital formation (% share of GDP)	18.5	18.0	18.9	17.0	15.7	15.1	15.0	15.0	15.4
Inflation rate	5.1	12.4	5.5	6.5	4.4	3.2	2.1	2.4	2.7
Productivity change (%)*	2.9	1.6	1.5	1.1	1.4	3.7	3.8	1.8	1.5
Real unit labour costs index	100.0	101.4	99.1	103.8	103.2	100.5	98.1	97.1	96.5
Employment annual change (%)	0.3	-0.2	1.8	-3.1	-1.9	-1.5	0.1	0.6	0.9
Unemployment rate (%)	1.9	6.9	9.0	8.8	10.1	10.4	9.6	8.8	8.4

*GDP at constant market prices per person employed.

Source: *European Economy 62,* 1996.

Mrs Thatcher's government was elected in 1979 and proceeded to act on radical economic ideas. That administration would undoubtedly claim the credit for the improved growth rate which followed, although growth was only at the EC average. *What is beyond doubt is that the depth of the recession in the early 1990s can be blamed on two UK government mistakes* (in the EU over this period there was a much milder recession).

By 1986, a rapidly rising balance of payments deficit demonstrated that demand was growing faster than the ability of UK firms to expand supplies, the gap being filled by imports. Nevertheless further huge increases in demand were to come. In the 1988 budget, large income tax cuts were supposed to lead to expanded output through increased incentives. Chancellor Lawson said in his budget speech

> '*The way to a strong economy is to boost incentives and enterprise. And that means, among other things, keeping income tax as low as possible. Excessive rates of income tax destroy enterprise.*'

There may be some truth in this proposition, but the tax changes expanded *aggregate demand* far more than they increased *aggregate supply*, thus raising prices – the rate of inflation – and sucking in even more imports.

To combat the surge in inflation, interest rates were progressively raised, from 7.5 per cent in May 1988 to 15 per cent in October 1989, at which extremely high level they stayed for the next twelve months. In October 1990 the interest rate was reduced by one percentage point and simultaneously the then Chancellor, John Major, *took sterling into the ERM at too high an exchange rate.* His successor as Chancellor, Norman Lamont, ended up trying to defend an overvalued pound at its ERM-fixed rate.

If a rate is to be maintained against the judgements of the markets, it has to be by increasing the rate of interest. *So interest rates remained high although the domestic economy desperately needed them to be reduced.* During the boom of 1986–88 firms and businesses had borrowed heavily, house prices had also boomed and many people had taken out large mortgages. Soon all were to find their repayments hugely swollen by the unexpectedly high interest rates. Consumers cut back their expenditures, investment fell, firms and businesses began to go bankrupt with consequent job losses, leading to further falls in demand. As many people lost their firms, businesses, jobs and homes the government maintained high interest rates to hold the exchange rate of sterling in the ERM.

Eventually, large-scale speculators realized that the sterling exchange rate could not be held and enormous capital flows began. The Prime Minister and the Chancellor of the Exchequer both made public announcements that the rate of exchange would be maintained. The ERM system permits countries in such a situation to agree a devaluation of their currencies, but despite promptings from other EU members the British government stubbornly refused to do this, preferring to pour huge sums into the foreign exchanges, at one time spending at the rate of £2 billion per hour, before having to admit ignominious defeat. One speculator, George Soros, made a profit of £650 million, while the losses made by the British government, on behalf of taxpayers, exceeded £4 billion.

Sterling was forced out of the ERM in September 1992. Subsequent reductions in interest rates were very welcome, but recovery from a recession of the depth which the government caused was slow.

- How does the UK compare with the EU average?

The account just given of the UK economy's performance makes it clear that membership of the EU is no panacea; it leaves much scope for national incompetence. But surely other governments are also less than perfect and the UK economy should not be examined in isolation. How does it compare with the EU average?

In 1960 the UK enjoyed a substantially higher **GDP per head** (income) than the average of the other members. By the time of accession the UK had lost this advantage. In the 1980s the relative position of the UK began to improve slightly, and in the late years of that decade GNP per head was 2–3 per cent above the EU average. Alas, the government's economic policies then caused the UK's relative position to plunge by 8 per cent between 1989 and 1991. As Table 10 shows, there has since been some improvement.

Table 10   GNP per head in the UK compared with EUR15
(EUR15 = 100)

1960	123.0
1970	103.7
1980	97.0
1990	100.0
1991	94.3
1992	95.3
1993	97.0
1994	96.7

Source: *European Economy 63,* 1997.

It is impossible to say how much of the credit or blame for the UK's relative economic performance lies with UK governments, and how much affect EU membership has had. However, if trends between 1960 and accession had continued to the present day, the UK's relative GDP would have fallen by now to be little over half that of our EU neighbours. *The fact that it is only slightly less than the EU average supports (but does not prove) the hypothesis that membership has been beneficial.*

The problem of agriculture
The much-criticized Common Agricultural Policy has had four major negative influences on the UK.

• Misallocation of resources
Agriculture has been much more heavily protected than the manufacturing sector, so significant **resource misallocation** has occurred. Resources used by agriculture could have been used more productively in other sectors. High food prices push up labour costs and reduce international competitiveness. Dumping food surpluses on world markets helps to reduce the costs of some competitors (Japan is a major

food importer), and makes other food exporters poorer – thus reducing their demand for UK and other EU exports.

• Trade diversion
Before accession the UK purchased food imports at low world market prices. Since accession, much food has been purchased from other member countries at the much higher internal prices. There has thus been **trade diversion**.

• Support costs
The budgetary cost of supporting European agriculture has fallen disproportionately heavily upon the UK. The UK had to contribute its share of this **support cost,** much of which paid for the disposal of agricultural surpluses produced by other members. *In the 1970s only the UK and Germany were net contributors to the budget.*

However, as the method of financing the EU budget has changed, and agricultural price support has declined in relative terms, other members have also become net contributors. As noted in Chapter 1, the EU budget now transfers income from richer to poorer members. Some aspects of the changing balance of net contributions can be seen in Table 11.

Table 11 Net contributions to the EU budget (million Ecus)

	1980	1988	1994	1995
Belgium	-273	-995	-307	-268
Denmark	334	351	188	353
Germany	-1 670	-6 107	-13 834	-12 941
Greece		1 492	3 813	3 438
Spain		1 334	3 006	7 440
France	380	-1 781	-2 801	-1 834
Ireland	687	1 159	1 727	1 724
Italy	681	124	-2 806	-1 250
Luxembourg	-5	-67	250	-42
Netherlands	395	1 150	-1 811	-1 794
Austria				-1 008
Portugal		515	1 881	2 327
Finland				-219
Sweden				-977
United Kingdom	-1 364	-2 070	-1 585	-5 023

Source: Derived from Court of Auditors annual reports.

Whether the benefits and burdens of the EU budget are fairly distributed is difficult to say.

- The *receipts* side is distorted because import duties are collected at the port of entry rather than in the country where they are consumed.
- Similarly, *payments* for the removal of agricultural surpluses may be made in countries other than those of the producing farmers.

In addition to these budgetary considerations, there are also real **resource transfers** because consumers in one member state are paying higher than world prices for food imported from other members.

- Environmental costs

High cereal prices persuaded farmers to plough much of the chalk downs, which at world prices would have remained in traditional grazing. So ancient grasslands rich in wildlife – flowers, butterflies, birds etc. – became cornfields whose production added to cereal surpluses. This is but one illustration of an extensive catalogue of unnecessary **environmental degradation** caused by the CAP's past high-price regime. Unfortunately it is very difficult to recapture lost habitats, and impossible to recreate lost species, so the reformed CAP does not represent a return to paradise lost.

Summary

How much the CAP has cost the UK is unknown. The four costs identified above are of three types. The simplest is that of budgetary transfers which are known. More difficult are the costs of trade diversion and resource misallocation which can only be estimated in relation to various assumptions. A further degree of difficulty is associated with estimating environmental costs – how can you value wild flowers, butterflies or a beautiful view? Politicians usually ignore all but the budgetary costs of the CAP, and take decisions related only to these.

Other environmental benefits

Environmental 'goods' and 'bads' are difficult to estimate, but they are very important to our welfare. On many of these issues common action is essential because action by individual nations is unlikely.

Acid rain is a good example. Its major source is coal-burning electricity power stations. Coal always contains some sulphur. When it is burnt, sulphurous gases enter the atmosphere appearing later in acid rain which corrodes public buildings (especially those built of limestone), acidifies lakes causing the death of fish, and harms large areas of pine forest in northern Europe. Removing sulphurous gases from power station smoke is expensive, and so increases the costs of generating electricity. No government will want to see its costs rise by unilaterally introducing desulphurization. The UK recently finished its first power station desulphurization plant as a result of EU rather than UK policy. Similarly, EU legislation is responsible for the UK cleaning up its drinking water and its beaches.

Conclusion: is membership of the EU a good thing?

At the time of writing the UK has been a member for nearly 25 years. Has membership been of net economic benefit so far, and what of the future?

Looking at the past, a conclusion is surprisingly difficult. The most widely known consequence of membership is the high budgetary cost of the CAP. Other costs and benefits are difficult to estimate. One pointer, already mentioned above, is that prior to membership the UK's GDP was growing much more slowly than the average for the Community, but has fared better since accession. Unfortunately such information is capable of very different interpretations; it might be argued, for example, that outside the Community the UK's relative economic decline could have been reversed more effectively. No definitive answer to these questions is possible.

It is, perhaps, too soon to attempt to assess whether membership of the Union is economically beneficial to the UK. The full benefits of the Single Market have not been achieved yet. But if the economic analysis of Chapter 2 is valid, then the UK will benefit in the long run, unless of course the UK becomes a depressed region which is a possibility raised by the analysis of Chapter 5.

KEY WORDS

Sovereignty	Support costs
GDP per head	Resource transfers
Resource misallocation	Environmental degradation
Trade diversion	Environmental benefits

Essay topics

1. 'More than 40 per cent of Japanese investment in Europe is based in Britain.' *The Independent*, 15 November 1995
   (a) Examine the factors which might explain why Britain is a relatively attractive location for corporate investment from Japan.
   [40 marks]
   (b) Analyse the economic benefits of this investment on (i) Britain's balance of payments, and (ii) employment and national income in Britain. [60 marks]
   [University of London Examinations and Assessment Council 1997]
2. Outline the arguments for and against European monetary union. Explain how the creation of a single currency and a European Central Bank could affect monetary policy in the UK. [25 marks]
   [Northern Examinations and Assessment Board 1996]

Data response question

The following task is based on a question set by the University of London Examinations and Assessment Council in 1997. Read the following article which is adapted from a piece by Bill Martin, 'Investment shortfall spells the end of Clarke's dream', published in the *Sunday Times* on 23 October 1994. Then answer the questions.

Economic recovery

Supporters of Britain's membership of the exchange rate mechanism (ERM) had believed that devaluation would result in a higher rate of inflation and have no lasting effect on the real economy. In fact, the economy's performance has bettered even the expectations of the few people who were optimistic about the effects of devaluation. Not only has there been a strong recovery and falling inflation, but there has also been a falling rate of unemployment and a reduced current account deficit.

Since sterling's exit from the ERM, the dole queue has shortened while the current account deficit has shrunk from an average of £10 billion a year to an annualised £4 billion in the first half of 1994.

Has the economic miracle finally arrived? Probably not. Leaving aside the question of accuracy of the (flattering) official figures, it is not pedantic to point out that the sharp fall in this year's current

---

account deficit owes much to freak jumps in oil production and overseas investment income. Without these, the external deficit was still about £17 billion a year, 2.5% of national income. That economic recovery should come with a stable, rather than larger, underlying current account deficit is still impressive and is explained by manufactured exports which, after two years of modest expansion, rose rapidly as a result of an improving world recovery and export profitability boosted by devaluation.

Alas, further progress will prove far from easy. The big export boost, on top of a consumer-led recovery now in its third year, has used up much of manufacturers' spare plant capacity. Capital utilisation rates in the summer were surprisingly high, not far below peaks seen in most business cycles, excluding the Lawson boom.

How is this possible after what appears to be such a slow recovery? The answer is straightforward: for more than a decade, manufacturers' investment has wholly failed to match the vast demands of the British consumer. Since 1979, estimates of manufacturers' capital stock show a small increase of only 5%. The volume of general consumer spending, by contrast, records a remarkable 40% rise.

1. Why did some economists consider that devaluation 'would result in a higher rate of inflation and have no lasting effect on the real economy'? [5 marks]
2. How could you explain the fact that devaluations did *not* result in a higher rate of inflation? [4 marks]
3. Under what circumstances would you expect devaluation to result in 'a falling rate of unemployment and a reduced current account deficit'? [6 marks]
4. (a) Examine *two* reasons why investment spending showed such a small increase after 1979. [4 marks]
   (b) Examine the economic implications of the differing rates of growth of capital stock and of general consumer spending.
   [6 marks]

Chapter Eight

Further enlargements to the south and east

'... any European State may apply to become a member ...'
Article 237 of the Treaty of Rome

In 1989 the collapse of communism in the USSR and its east European satellites took both East and West by surprise. The central and east European countries (**CEECs** or **transitional economies**) wished to become free market democracies, but after decades of dictatorship and central planning the transition was clearly going to be slow and difficult. The immediate problem was how to develop free market and democratic institutions in countries which for several decades had experience of neither.

The CEECs looked to the EU for help, and the Community responded positively. *Obviously it is in the EU's interest to support the development of stable, politically and economically sympathetic countries as its neighbours.* Soon the CEECs decided that their futures would be best assured as members of the EU, and so far ten have applied to join: Bulgaria, the Czech Republic, Estonia, Hungary, Latvia, Lithuania, Poland, Romania, Slovakia and Slovenia. To the south, Turkey, Cyprus and Malta have long wished to join. This chapter considers the problems of such further enlargements.

Economic and political perspectives for the CEECs
The CEECs' combined population and land area are about one-third of those of the **EUR15** (see Figure 4), but their combined GDP is of the order of just one twenty-fifth (i.e. 4 per cent) of that of the EUR15. Before these countries can be accepted as full EU members their economies need to be competitive, with wages close to the EU average, otherwise the free movement of labour permitted within the EU would result in a huge westward migration of CEEC peoples seeking better working and living conditions.

The economic disparities are too large to be removed quickly, and the challenge for the EU is to encourage and assist economic reform in the applicant countries under some arrangement which falls far short of full membership in the near future. Yet the aspirations of the CEECs must be recognized and catered for if political stability in the region is to be assured.

Changes are also needed within the EU before the accession of the CEECs. Most notably, further reform of the CAP is essential. The extension of the existing CAP to countries where agriculture is still the occupation of around a quarter of the labour force would be extremely expensive.

What about the former USSR? The Russians are European, but most of the other ex-USSR countries are Asian. The combined populations of Russia, Ukraine and Georgia are equal to about 50 per cent of the current EUR15. Such a huge Russian-speaking bloc is far larger than any other group in the EU, which means that this is one region of Europe that is unlikely ever to join.

Instead, the USSR (minus Estonia, Latvia and Lithuania) has been replaced by a looser organization – the **Commonwealth of Independent States** (CIS). The EU provides aid via the 'technical assistance to the CIS' (**TACIS**) programme. Under this, EU expertise is offered to smooth the transition from centrally planned to market economies, and for the reform of public administration, social services, education, environmental projects, and (not least) nuclear safety. TACIS expenditure totalled 2.3 billion Ecus in the period 1991–95 and is likely to expand considerably.

The PHARE programme

In 1989 the Community negotiated trade and cooperation agreements with *individual* CEECs. These agreements reduced progressively the EU quota and tariff barriers.

PHARE (Pologne, Hungrie, assistance pour la restructuration économique) is a financial instrument set up in 1989 to provide technical assistance for economic restructuring – initially for Poland and Hungry, but later extended to all CEECs. By 1996 the Community had committed 5 billion Ecus to this programme, a figure that is expected to rise to 11 billion Ecus by the end of the decade.

Some of this expenditure has taken the form of grants for improving infrastructure. This has a **multiplier effect,** for example by stimulating investments by the European Investment Bank. Investments have also been encouraged through the European Bank for Reconstruction and Development.

Europe Agreements

These are **association agreements** designed to prepare the CEECs for eventual full membership of the EU. Starting in 1991, they gradually

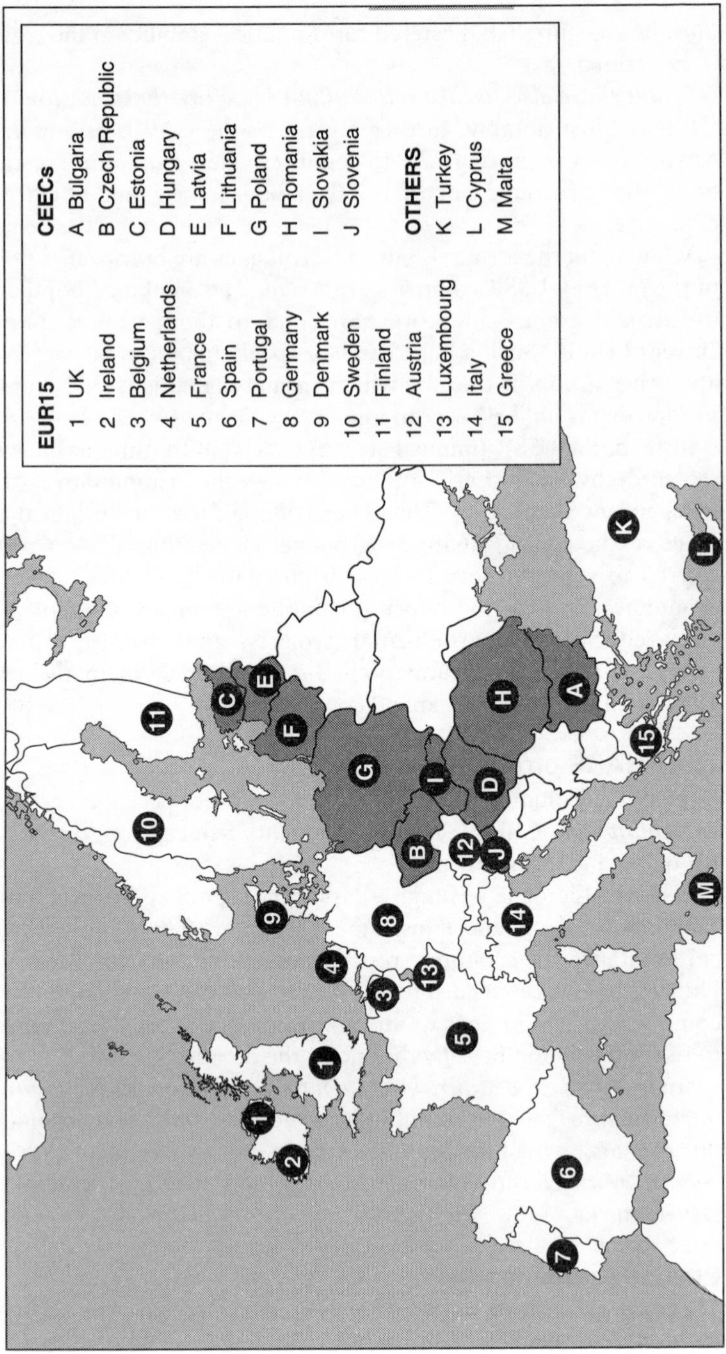

Figure 4 The present and possible future of the European Union

EUR15
1 UK
2 Ireland
3 Belgium
4 Netherlands
5 France
6 Spain
7 Portugal
8 Germany
9 Denmark
10 Sweden
11 Finland
12 Austria
13 Luxembourg
14 Italy
15 Greece

CEECs
A Bulgaria
B Czech Republic
C Estonia
D Hungary
E Latvia
F Lithuania
G Poland
H Romania
I Slovakia
J Slovenia

OTHERS
K Turkey
L Cyprus
M Malta

replaced the original trade and cooperation arrangements, and by 1996 each of the ten CEECs noted above had signed the new agreements. Their long-term function is gradually to align the CEECs' economic and legal systems with those of the EU. Immediate measures towards this end are:

- opening up of free trade
- provision of technical assistance
- establishment of closer economic dialogue
- establishment of political dialogue.

The CEECs were eager to become full members as soon as possible and probably underestimated the difficulties, but the EU has proceeded slowly. It took until 1993, at the Copenhagen Council, for the heads of governments to confirm that applicant CEECs could join as soon as they fulfilled the economic and political requirements for membership.

Under the Europe Agreements, trade in manufactures was to be liberalized slowly – the CEECs were to remove all barriers against EU goods within ten years. The EU was to remove its barriers against the CEECs' products more rapidly, except for a list of sensitive items for which the CEECs might have a comparative advantage – coal, steel, textiles and agricultural products. The EU has been much criticized for restricting trade in these 'sensitive' products, most economists believing that the substantial welfare gains from trade liberalization would have been at little cost to EU producers.

Despite these restrictions, most of the trade in *industrial goods* was rapidly liberalized and the CEECs enjoyed a major shift in trade, both imports and exports, towards the EU. *Agricultural products* remain an anomaly: CEEC exports have been discriminated against by the EU, and the CAP's export subsidy system has resulted in the CEECs (with the exception of Hungary) becoming net food importers from the EU.

Accession negotiations

The EU Intergovernmental Conference started in 1997 is dealing mainly with internal affairs, concentrating on EMU and the need to improve further the efficiency of decision-making. However, the Conference is also preparing the ground for further enlargement, and negotiations with the Czech Republic, Estonia, Hungary, Poland and Slovenia are planned for spring 1998. These talks could be very lengthy – perhaps like those for the accession of Spain and Portugal which meandered on for seven years. After accession there will be **transition periods** which, even for the most advanced of the CEECs, are certain to be at least five years. When the other five CEECs are likely to be judged ready for accession negotiations is unclear.

Meanwhile the EU has plenty to do to prepare for the accession of new members. Ultimately its policies and decision-making machinery must be modified to accommodate them and answers to the following questions must be found:

- How is the weighted majority voting system to be changed?
- How are portfolios to be organized in a much larger Community?
- How can the CAP be reformed to cope with the accession of countries where agriculture is backward but extremely important?

Accessions of Turkey, Cyprus and Malta

Turkey negotiated an association agreement with the Community in 1963 and was at that time expected to become a member during the 1990s. However, the Commission published an opinion in 1989 which effectively postponed negotiations indefinitely. The reason given was that Turkey had a large and rapidly expanding population, a weak economy and lower living standards than any part of the Community. Finally, the Turkish invasion of Cyprus, which resulted in the partition of the island into a Turkish north and Greek south, means that at least one current EU member would veto Turkish accession.

Cyprus negotiated an association agreement in 1972 and applied in 1990 for full membership. The continuing division of the island has prevented further progress, but Cyprus is to be included in the 1998 accession negotiations.

Malta has had an association agreement since 1970 and also applied in 1990 for full membership.

Conclusion

Further enlargements are certain to follow the achievement of EMU. However, before this is possible substantial adjustments are required on both sides. The EU needs to reform the CAP and to alter its decision-making machinery to cope with a large number of new members. The applicants need to adjust their markets and political institutions towards EU systems. For the CEECs this will be difficult, and even with EU help the process will be slow.

```
┌─────────────────────────────────────────────────────────┐
│                      KEY WORDS                          │
│                                                         │
│   CEECs                       PHARE                     │
│   EUR15                       Multiplier effect         │
│   Commonwealth of             Association agreements     │
│      Independent States (CIS) Transition periods        │
│   TACIS                       Transition economies      │
│                                                         │
└─────────────────────────────────────────────────────────┘
```

Essay topics

1. (a) In what ways has economic integration already occurred in the European Union? [12 marks]
   (b) Assess the economic issues involved in determining the future form of economic integration in the European Union. [13 marks]
   [University of Cambridge Local Examinations Syndicate 1996]
2. (a) Examine the economic benefits which Austria, Sweden and Finland may have hoped to gain by joining the European Union in 1995. [60 marks]
   (b) What economic issues are likely to arise from the further expansion of the EU to include countries in eastern Europe? [40 marks]
   [University of London Examinations and Assessment Council 1997]

Data response question

The following task is based on a question set by the University of Cambridge Local Examinations Syndicate in 1997. Study all the information given below and then answer the questions.

```
┌─────────────────────────────────────────────────────────┐
│                                                         │
│   Hungary: forging closer links with the European Union │
│                                                         │
│   Hungary was the first of the former Eastern bloc      │
│   economies to open its doors to free trade and today   │
│   is the only one which has completely liberalized its  │
│   import trade. This commitment to free trade is one of │
│   the credentials which will stand it in good stead to  │
│   gain EU membership. Table A shows certain aspects of  │
│   Hungary's trade from 1991 to 1994.                    │
│                                                         │
└─────────────────────────────────────────────────────────┘
```

Table A Basic statistics of Hungarian–EU trade, 1991–94

	1991	1992	1993	1994
Total trade				
Hungarian exports				
(Ft* billion current prices)	764	844	820	772
Hungarian imports				
(Ft billion current prices)	844	879	1163	1157
Export/import ratio (%)	91	96	71	67
Trade with the EU				
Hungarian exports				
(Ft billion current prices)	350	419	381	359
Hungarian imports				
(Ft billion current prices)	352	375	466	462
Export/import ratio (%)	99	112	82	78
Other information				
Exchange rate *v* US$ (Jan. 1993 = 100)	93	95	100.7	113
External debt (US$ billion)	na	na	24.6	28.5
Debt ratio (years)†	na	na	1.6	2.0
% change in consumer prices	18	20	23	19

*Ft (Forint) is the Hungarian unit of currency.
†The number of years of hard currency income required to repay debt.

1. (a) Why are imports measured at 'current prices'? [1 mark]
   (b) Explain an alternative way by which the value of imports might be measured. [2 marks]
2. (a) From Table A, compare the export/import ratio of total trade with the export/import ratio of Hungary's trade with the EU.
   [2 marks]
   (b) Explain the implications of any differences you have observed.
   [2 marks]
3. (a) In the period shown, was the Hungarian currency appreciating or depreciating with respect to the US$? Explain your answer.
   [2 marks]
   (b) What might be the economic implications of this for the Hungarian economy? [2 marks]
4. Suppose you are a UK consumer goods manufacturer seeking to set up a production plant in Hungary. Explain how the data in Table A might be useful to you. [4 marks]
5. Comment on the economic implications of the debt problems facing the Hungarian economy. [5 marks]

Conclusion

All for one and one for all – Dumas

When one now observes the progress of economic and political integration in the European Union, it is difficult to believe that just over 50 years ago most of its members were in the depths of the Second World War. That war involved the four largest EU members as some of the main antagonists, two on one side, two on the other. It was separated from a similar preceding war by only one generation. If the coming together in the European Union of these previously warring factions had no other effect than to prevent a further war, the Union would be a great economic success – for even ignoring the terrible human costs, the economic waste of those two wars was enormous.

The prevention of war seems a rather negative benefit; this chapter now looks at the positive side where 'all for one and one for all' is becoming literally true through the process of economic integration. We must look at the economic progress which has been achieved and the prospects for further progress in a Europe of rapid and accelerating change.

The economic success of the EU

During the past 30 years the economies of the fifteen (EUR15) have grown more rapidly than that of the USA. As Table 12 shows, in 1960 the GDP per head in the USA was 80 per cent higher than that in the EU, but by 1996 the American lead was reduced to about 40 per cent.

Table 12 GDP per head: EUR15 compared* with USA and Japan, 1960–96 (EUR15=100)

	USA	Japan
1960	180.7	55.7
1970	156.7	91.5
1980	143.5	99.0
1990	138.7	112.5
1995	140.8	116.1
1997 (forecast)	140.1	117.9

*The comparison is in terms of purchasing power parity.
Source: *European Economy 63*, 1997.

Over the same period, Japanese GDP per head has rocketed from being 55 per cent of that in the EU to gaining a lead of nearly 18 per cent. The report on European economic progress must be 'fairly good but could do better!'.

Economic growth has been very variable during the Community's first four decades. Table 13 shows that initially growth was rapid, but worldwide recessions, largely caused by oil price shocks in 1974 and again in 1979, greatly reduced growth, and led to the under-employment of resources in general and labour in particular. After 1984 growth began to accelerate, but unemployment remained high compared with the 1960s.

The improvements in the 1980s can be attributed to three main factors:

- success in controlling inflation
- the implementation of supply-side policies
- introduction of the Single Market.

As described in Chapter 3, there are still some non-tariff barriers – notably differences in tax rates and excise duties – distorting competition and hindering the operation of comparative advantage. But these factors are not sufficient to explain the slowdown since the beginning of the 1990s: economic growth has slowed, and unemployment has risen. The Commission blames an undeserved loss of confidence. Within Europe the 1990 German reunification was far more expensive than expected, and simultaneously the recession in the UK rapidly deepened. It is probable that such problems in two of the largest economies of the Union have been significant factors in the slowdown which has affected all.

Table 13 EUR15: some economic indicators, 1961–96.

	1961 –73	1974 –85	1986 –90	1991	1992	1993	1994	1995	1996 (forecast)
Growth of GDP (real annual %)	4.7	2.0	3.3	1.5	1.0	-0.6	2.8	2.5	1.5
Gross investment as % of GDP	23.4	21.3	20.3	20.9	20.2	18.9	18.7	18.9	18.9
Employment change (annual %)	0.3	0	1.3	0.1	-1.4	-1.9	-0.3	0.6	0.2
Inflation rate	5.2	10.5	4.9	5.5	4.5	3.7	2.7	3.0	2.6
Unemployment (%)	2.3	6.4	9.0	8.3	9.4	10.9	11.3	10.9	11.0

Source: *European Economy 62,* 1996.

Appraisal of EU economic strategy

Since the early days of the Community the Commission has been formulating long-term plans. This is in marked contrast to the UK government's attitude prevalent from 1979 to 1997; here, investment decisions have been regarded as the sole perogative of firms and businesses operating in a free market. The 1996 EU budget provided over 3 billion Ecus (about £2 billion) for research and development, concentrated particularly on high-technology areas. Is such public intervention in research more effective (in terms of economic growth) than leaving it to industry?

The experiences of Japan and the USA provide some pointers. Japanese leadership in many areas of technology has resulted from many years of public intervention, with huge expenditures being targeted on correctly identified growth areas. High growth rates in the USA since the Second World War have been attributed to civil spin-offs from gigantic military research programmes – for example, the original Boeing airliner, the first major successful jet airliner, came from a very expensively developed military aircraft. The slower USA growth rate of the 1990s correlates with the rapid reduction of military research expenditures, *suggesting that the market alone is not the best deliverer of economic growth even in the most capitalistic of cultures.*

Welfare

It is a truism that money cannot buy happiness. Neither can GNP per head fully measure economic welfare. GNP excludes many things which we tend to take for granted but which are important to our wellbeing – peace, security, plentiful food supplies, freedom and democracy. There is little doubt that in an uncertain world the size and strength of the EU more effectively protects these matters, which are fundamental to our welfare, than individual nations acting separately. Perhaps this is the real reason why both prosperous and poor countries continue to be attracted to the EU.

Conclusion

The European Union has developed from its original six members to nine, to ten, to twelve, to fifteen and still more countries wish to join. Clearly in the eyes of many the Union is a success. The continuing development of the Single Market promises to further enhance the Union's economy – already it is the world's largest developed country market in terms of population, and as Adam Smith observed, 'specialization is limited by the extent of the market' – meaning that efficiency depends on market size. The EU has the potential to become, within a generation, the world's major economic power.

The Maastricht Treaty (TEU) attempts to further the process of making 'all into one' by emphasizing political integration as well as economic integration. Indeed the former is essential to the progress of economic and monetary union. But there is a conflict between this deepening of the current Union and its widening to include the much poorer CEECs. Reconciling these conflicts will be the major challenge of the next decade and beyond.

Index